Dr. Dunbar's
GOOD LITTLE DOG BOOK

Dr. Dunbar's
GOOD LITTLE DOG BOOK

A Puppy Training Guide
for the Television Videos
"Training the Companion Dog"
& "Training Dogs With Dunbar"

based on
Dr. Dunbar's
SIRIUS® Puppy Training

James & Kenneth
PUBLISHERS

Dr. Dunbar's GOOD LITTLE DOG BOOK
© 2003 Ian Dunbar

Third Edition published in 2003 by:

James & Kenneth Publishers
2140 Shattuck Avenue #2406
Berkeley, California 94704
1-800-784-5531

First published in 1992 by Spillers Pet Foods
Second Edition in 1996 by James & Kenneth Publishers

Printed in the United States of America

IBSN 1-888047-02-X

For the dogs:
Ashby, Phoenix, and Oso

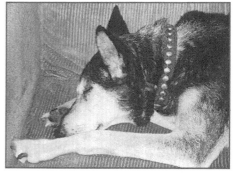

Ashby

Phoenix

*Since the second edition
was written, Ashby and
Phoenix have died,
and Oso has grown old,
but he still enjoys his
sunset years.*

Oso

Filming puppy classes at Newhouse

Photo Credits
Anonymous: page 126
Linda Carlson: pages 5, 36, and back cover
Dolphin Experience: page 19
Jamie Dunbar: pages 10, 68, 69, 72, 83, 86, 87, and 90
Nancy Hachmeister: page 169
Wayne Hightower: page 13
Mimi Whei Ping Lou: page 103
Neal Morrison: page 55
Carmen Noradunghian: pages 18 and 150
Sue Pearson: page 12
Spillers Pet Foods: pages 6, 8, 9, 108, and front cover
Diana Robinson: pages 20, 33, 58, 59, 62, 63, 70, 71, 74, 76, 77, 78, 80, 81, 82, 93, and 159
Lesley Spanton: page 106

All other photographs were taken by the author.

Front Cover Design by Quark & Bark Late Night Graphics Co.
Back Cover Design by Montessaurus Media.

Contents

Filming "Dogs With Dunbar"...

with author
Jilly Cooper,

actress
Liza Goddard,

and actress/author
Alexandra Bastedo.

Newhouse in the New Forest

This little book was written with so many good memories of wonderful summers in England with the Ark Production team, filming the "Dogs With Dunbar" television series at Newhouse in the New Forest. Warm woofs and happy wags to all involved: to Director Steve "Guinness" Ray and Producer Veronica Charlwood (I am especially indebted to Veronica— thank you Veronica!), to the camera crew, to Pam and Yvonne at Ark Productions, to Clive at TVS, to Mary at Spillers (who make the munchies for the dogs), and especially to the real stars—the wonderful puppies and their wonderful owners.

Rather than trying to act like a dog, it is easier, and much more practical, to teach dogs to understand our language.

CHAPTER ONE

Get Ahead of the Pack
And the View Will Improve!

So Joe Pup has come to live with you! Now what? Basically, you are at a fork in the road. Living with a dog can be a joy, or a pain. The success of the future relationship depends on you teaching your puppydog the rules and regulations of domestic living. The most important time in a dog's life is right now. First impressions are so very important for all dogs, and especially for puppies. Consequently, the next few weeks are crucial to doggy development. A little help and guidance at this stage will have a profound and long-lasting effect, which will enrich the doggy-human relationship for years to come. So don't delay, train today!

Why Train?

Let's begin by asking ourselves, "Why train?" Well, training is really just another means of communicating with and better understanding a non-verbal creature, be it a pet dog, a pre-verbal child, or a partially-verbal sibling or spouse.

Our best friend—the domestic dog—is a social animal. It would be inconsiderate and antisocial not to train it. How else could we communicate with each other? By learning doggy lingo? Would it not be impractical to try to communicate with our dog via urine marks, ear positions, and tail wags? Anyway, few humans could ever master the many nuances of the various dog languages. Luckily, though, dogs can easily learn our language, if only we teach them! Basically, dog training comprises teaching dogs ESL—English as a Second Language—so that our dogs will understand human words for doggy behaviors and actions.

Dogs cannot read dog training books. Therefore, we need to teach them our household rules, basic manners, and social etiquette; otherwise they will live by doggy rules, and paw, and sniff, and pee when saying hello.

Remember, we are asking dogs to live with us—in our domestic environment, and according to our customs and rules. Consequently, it is only fair for us to teach dogs how to avoid causing offense to family, friends, or any members of the general public with whom they may come into contact—especially non-dog owners. It is no good for us to have strict doggy rules but then keep them a secret from our dogs.

A well-trained dog can be a joy to live with: a household companion with whom to share our day; an enthusiastic and attentive greeter to always welcome us home; a furry psychologist to listen to our woes with an expression of sympathetic concern; a catalyst to go for walks and keep fit and healthy; and above all, a snuggly warm mass to cuddle on the couch. However, these benefits do not come by magic. Children and parents alike must realize that cartoon dogs are fantasy, and that Lassie, Benji, and Eddie were all highly trained animals. (In fact, Lassie was several highly trained animals.) For your dog to become a well-behaved and an enjoyable family pet, it too must be trained and socialized.

And why not train your dog? The training game can be a lot of fun. Just one look at our videos and television programs and you can see both owners and dogs are wagging their tails and obviously having the time of their lives. Why not learn how to have fun with your dog? And why not let your dog have some fun with you? Using the methods in this book, it is possible to enjoy training your dog while snuggling on the couch, reading romance novels, watching television, taking dog walks in the town or countryside, playing in the park, or picnicking on the beach.

Sadly, many dog owners are hesitant about training their dogs. Certainly, much antipathy towards training stems from the catastrophic influence of the last century's Trainers from The Dark Side. Many people think that training is a drag because in the twentieth century, dog training *was* a drag. There were just too many jerks at both ends of the leash. Far too many trainers treated their best friend like their worst enemy. So much so, in fact, that some owners still suffer the misassumption that it is necessary to dominate their dog and force it to obey: to squish the little sucker into a sit, to demand de-motivated downs, or to subject the poor dog to chained-collar heeling from Hell.

Not so! With the many recent advances and innovations in dog training techniques, force-methods are simply not necessary. Neither do they work that well in real-life settings. Moreover, although force-methods may have some short-term gains (although I can not think of any off-hand), there are many long-term losses—namely, the dog's reliability of performance, its good temperament, its confidence and trust in its owner, and ultimately the owner's peace of mind.

When owners incorporate excessive corrections or punishments into a training program, many dogs quickly develop Jekyll & Hyde—type personalities. Rather than learning what the trainer is trying to teach, the dog simply learns the times and situations when it need not obey because it cannot be punished. Whereas a dog might grudgingly comply when forced to do so and when punishment is imminent, it's a

Eddie

13

whole different story when the dog is off-leash, out of reach, or left at home unsupervised. In particular, off-leash reliability suffers badly and the dog develops a variety of owner-absent misbehaviors.

Punishment often creates additional problems. Repeated punishment may make your dog fearful and aggressive. And with too many corrections, the dog may grow to dislike its trainer (i.e., you!) as much as it dislikes training.

It is kinder and smarter by far to teach your dog how to enjoy acting like a dog in a fashion that is both appropriate and acceptable to you. For example, you can teach your dog where to pee and poop (in its indoor or outdoor doggy toilet), what to chew (chewtoys), when to bark (in response to the doorbell), when to jump up (on request for a hug), and when to pull on leash (to help you walk up steep hills).

Smarter yet is to teach your dog to comply with your wishes happily and willingly, by luring your dog to do what you want, and then rewarding it handsomely. Indeed, dog-friendly dog training focuses on teaching your dog to *want* to do what you want it to do.

Establish the Status Quo Right Away

Establish good habits from the outset. Remember, good habits are just as hard to break as bad habits!

The way your dog is allowed to behave during the first couple of weeks at home will set the precedent for many months and years to come. Consequently, you must take the time to teach your dog the rules of its new household, or it will improvise and develop rules of its own.

Even though your puppy is small, cute, and cuddly, you should imagine it as an adult and treat it accordingly. It would be unfair and inhumane to allow or encourage your pup to behave in a manner for which it might be punished later in life. For example, it would be cruel to allow the pup to jump up—let alone pet it when it does so— only to punish it for doing the same thing when it grows up. If you don't want your dog to jump up, pull on leash, bark excessively, or soil the house as an adult, then don't allow your puppy to indulge in these activities. Time invested now—teaching the required standards of behavior—will save months of misery for you and your dog later on. Establish an acceptable status quo from the outset and your dog will happily act this way as an adult.

Remember, though, behavior is always changing—sometimes for the better, sometimes for the worse. Basically, things improve if you work with your dog, and things often get worse if you don't. Both behavior and temperament tend to stabilize once the dog has reached its second or third birthday. Nonetheless, always be alert for the development of unwanted behaviors and quickly nip incipient problems in the bud. Do not dilly-dally, otherwise new problems will quickly develop into hard-to-break habits.

Training Priorities

Many people consider dog training to be synonymous with obedience and teaching basic manners. However, for pet dogs, socialization, developing bite-inhibition, and learning household etiquette are all much more important and far more urgent.

SIRIUS® Puppy Training classes at Citizen Canine in Oakland, California

Socialization and Bite Inhibition

It is easy to socialize a puppy. However, keeping an adolescent dog socialized requires frequent walks and frequent visits to dog parks.

Certainly, basic manners are very important and play a prominent role in the prevention and treatment of many behavior and temperament problems. However, specific socialization, bite inhibition, and temperament training exercises during puppyhood are far more important for a pet dog. Whereas it is possible (albeit a bit of a pain) to live with a dog with no manners, it is a bigger pain to live with a dog that has no bite inhibition and lacks confidence around family and friends, especially children.

Teaching bite inhibition and socializing your puppy to people are the most important items on its educational agenda. Your pup needs to be introduced to a wide variety of people—especially children, men, and strangers. Your pup needs to experience all the possible settings and situations it is likely to encounter as an adult dog, including meeting a wide variety of other dogs. Puppies that grow up to like other dogs and people can be a dream, whereas fearful and/or antisocial dogs can be a nightmare.

Socializing your puppy and teaching it to inhibit the force of its bites are both developmentally sensitive priorities and must be accomplished during early puppyhood. The narrow time-window for optimal socialization will begin to close by the time your pup is just twelve weeks old. Additionally, your puppy must develop a soft mouth before it is four-and-a-half months old.

Socializing a young puppy is easy and enjoyable. Socializing a fearful adolescent or adult dog is extremely time-consuming and heart-breaking. Teaching a young puppy to inhibit the force of its bites can be time-consuming and frustrating, but it is absolutely essential! Attempting to teach bite inhibition to an adolescent or adult dog is difficult, time-consuming, and potentially dangerous. Prevention is the key. Establish good habits from the outset. *Good habits are just as hard to break as bad habits!*

Household Etiquette

Teaching basic manners is a pressing item in your puppy's educational curriculum. However, much more urgent is your pup's education regarding household etiquette. In particular, your pup needs to be taught how to express its doggy nature in an appropriate way. Your pup needs to learn acceptable outlets for its normal, natural, and necessary canine behaviors, such as *where* to relieve itself, *what* to chew, *where* to dig, and *when* (and for how long) to bark. Puppies must especially be taught how to idle away the many hours of the day when left at home alone.

Your puppy needs to learn where to relieve itself and what to chew.

17

Adolescent dogs with no respect for house or garden tend to wear thin their welcome. Misbehaving dogs are usually abandoned or surrendered to animal shelters. Indeed, predictable and preventable behavior problems are the most common terminal illnesses for pet dogs.

Preventing the development of highly predictable behavior problems is just so easy. Breaking established bad habits can be quite time-consuming. Prevention is the key. Establish good habits from the outset. *Good habits are just as hard to break as bad habits!*

Good Manners

Your puppy needs to be schooled in good manners and learn how to act around people: specifically, to sit when greeting people, to settle down when requested, and to walk calmly on leash.

Using lure/reward techniques, it is easy to train your puppydog at any age. However, lure/reward training techniques are just so easy, and so much fun, you may as well start training your puppy right away. There is simply nothing as thrilling as watching a young pup learn to come, sit, lie down, and roll over in its very first lesson. A puppy's attentiveness, eagerness, and exuberance for the training game are truly astounding. It is time to show off your puppy to family, friends, and neighbors.

Your puppy's attention will begin to wander as it approaches adolescence and develops adult doggy interests. Getting a head start on your puppy's education will make it much easier to control your puppy's rambunctious behavior as it weathers the social storm of adolescence. Prevention is the key. Establish good habits from the outset. *Good habits are just as hard to break as bad habits!*

The lure/reward method described in this book is not limited to training puppies. On the contrary, since this book was first published, lure/reward techniques have become the method of choice for rehabilitating fearful and aggressive dogs, and for instructing good-natured, but otherwise uneducated, adult dogs.

Lure/reward methods are *de rigeur* for training lions, tigers, killer whales, and grizzly bears. Over a century ago, similar off-leash techniques were the accepted practice for training dogs and puppies. Unfortunately, they were replaced with a harsher regime of laborious, on-leash, push-pull, squish-squash, narrow-brained methods. With most dogs it is unnecessary to use force. With many dogs it is counterproductive. Why treat your best friend like an adversary in the domestic training arena? Welcome back to lure/reward training—the historically-proven, so-old-that-it-is-new-again, commonsense, natural, easy and enjoyable way to train your puppydog.

Lure/reward methods are de rigeur *for training pigs, parrots, polar bears, killer whales, and dolphins. Why do we discriminate against dogs (and horses)? Don't dogs deserve to be taught using the same fun methods?*

Lure...

...and reward.

CHAPTER TWO

E's of Lure/Reward Training

Lure/reward pet dog training techniques are Efficient, Effective, Easy, Efficacious, Enjoyable, and Expedient. Compared with trying to train using corrections and punishments, lure/reward techniques require less owner effort to produce much quicker and more reliable doggy results.

Efficient

Lure/reward methods take less time than trying to train using corrections and punishments. By nature, lure/reward training is much more efficient than punishment-training. Whereas there are an infinite number ways for the dog to get it wrong (which require an infinite number of punishments), there is only one right way! So in terms of your time-investment and your dog's speed of learning, it is far better to show your dog exactly what is required and to reward it for complying, than it is to attempt the impossible—trying to punish the dog for each and every mistake.

Housetraining is a fine example. The average dog could think of an infinite number of choice locations to empty its bladder and bowels in the space of a 200-square-foot living room alone. Since the dog could make an infinite number of mistakes, correcting the problem would require an infinite number of corrections, and hence an infinite amount of time. Punishment-training is like the Myth of Sisyphus—an everlastingly laborious and theoretically impossible task.

On the other hand, I can think only of one appropriate place for my dogs to relieve themselves—in the P Zone (underneath the plum tree at the bottom of the garden). Consequently, using lure/reward methods, housetraining becomes a quick and easy process. All we have to do is show our dog where we would like it to relieve itself, and then praise and reward it for doing so.

The same principle applies to other potential behavior problems like chewing, digging, and barking. Teach your dog what to chew, where to dig, and when to bark, and then reward it for doing so. We may extend the same principle to teaching manners. Rather than punishing a dog for jumping up, teach it to sit when greeting people and to jump up only when requested to "Give a Hug!"

There is an additional reason that punishment-training takes more time: the trainer has to wait for the dog to misbehave before it can be punished. Now if that isn't just too silly for words, I don't know what is. Aside from being decidedly unfair to provide the dog with no education and then punish it for breaking rules it never knew existed, what a ridiculous delay in training—to fiddle about and wait around for transgressions from an untrained dog. Why not be proactive and just teach your dog how you would like it to behave? Lure/reward training allows you to take the initiative and teach your dog what you would like it to do before it is forced to improvise and make mistakes. In fact, with correct management, lure/reward housetraining and chewtoy training can be virtually errorless.

Phoenie says, "Training must be efficient. If training is a big time-investment, people won't be bothered, and dogs will be deprived of their education. Dogs won't learn to understand English as a Second Language. Dogs won't be able to understand their owners. Dogs won't learn house rules and domestic etiquette, and so dogs will be forced to make up their own rules and act like dogs. And then their human companions will become upset. And that's not good! Training has to be efficient."

Effective

Dog training techniques must work: that is, they must be effective. Otherwise training would be a waste of time.

Punishment-training is relatively ineffective for pet dog training. People are just too inconsistent for punishment-training techniques to work in the domestic setting.

Many dog books emphasize consistency as the hallmark of successful training. Consistency is essential if one attempts to enforce household rules and manners using correction and punishment. For punishment-training to be effective, the dog must be punished each and every time it misbehaves. Now, apart from being a lot of work, this is actually impossible in most households. People are simply not 100% consistent 100% of the time. Certainly people can concentrate for short periods, but not all the time. Even when people try their hardest to concentrate for limited periods, their attention often wanders.

The myth of successful punishment-training comes from scientific research. Animal learning theory evolved from literally thousands of experiments involving millions of laboratory rats and pigeons, many of which were effectively trained using punishment-training (plain and simple punishment, aversive conditioning, and avoidance learning). In the laboratory experiments, the animals' behavior was monitored by electronic and mechanical sensors and punishment (usually electric shock) was automatic, or administered by computer.

Although punishment-training works extremely well in the laboratory, where animals are trained by tirelessly consistent computers, punishment-training is notoriously ineffective when people train animals, or when people teach people. In fact, were unfortunate dogs not abused in the process, punishment-training would be one huge joke.

Aside from being a colossal effort, and not working particularly well in practice, punishment-training has yet another major drawback. The dog only has to misbehave without being punished once to learn that there are occasions when it will not be punished for doing what it likes. This creates a multitude of problems, including owner-absent behavior problems, owner-present but functionally-absent problems, and owner physically-present but mentally-absent problems.

1. Owner-Absent Problems
The dog learns it would be a mite foolhardy to act like a dog when its owner is present, and so it intelligently waits for its owner to leave before indulging its basic doggy nature. The dog learns to enjoy expressing its normal, natural, and necessary doggy behavior (usually in a manner which owners consider to be inappropriate and annoying) when the owner is physically absent (out of the room, or away from home). Thus, punishment is often a primary motivator for owner-absent housesoiling, chewing, digging, and barking. In a sense, the so-called "treatment" is the cause.

2. Owner-Present but Functionally-Absent Problems
The dog learns it cannot be punished for misbehaving when it is off-leash and out of reach, or when the owner cannot respond (chatting on the telephone, taking a shower, cooking at the stove, feeding the baby, talking to someone on the street, or driving a car). To make matters worse, these are all extremely inconvenient times for your dog to act up and misbehave.

3. Owner Physically-Present but Mentally-Absent Problems
Dogs quickly learn to discern those times when their owners are mentally absent, and not paying attention. The less said about this the better.

But now the good news! Whereas consistency is absolutely essential for punishment-training to be effective, there is no need to be consistent when lure/reward training. In fact, inconsistency can actually be advantageous when rewarding a dog. Whenever your dog complies with your wishes, you may reward it if, and when, you like. Distribute the rewards whenever the fancy takes you—totally at random, if you like. You don't have to reward your dog every time. Isn't that just wickedly *wunderbar?*

Consider, for example, the allure of a one-armed bandit (slot machine), which dispenses a variety of rewards at random, compared with the dull predictability of an ATM, or a food vending machine, which pays out all the time (or at least is meant to). It may seem strange, but we humans will actually work harder and longer for fewer rewards if the rewards are unpredictable. Nothing spoils a dog more quickly, or devalues rewards in training, than handing out rewards willy nilly for every remotely correct response. What's more, when the dog is rewarded all the time, it takes only one response without reward for the critter to go on strike. One failed attempt to get food out of a vending machine and we assume it's broken. We stop trying. Similarly, one unrewarded "Sit" and your dog surmises, "Ahhhh Hah! I don't think she has a reward to give me," and the dog stops trying.

So adopt the slot machine approach. Make the handouts appear to be unpredictable, so your dog learns it is not uncommon for a number of unrewarded trials to be followed by a big payout. Vary the frequency, type, and amount of praise and rewards and you'll find your dog will gladly oblige without having to be rewarded each time. This puts you in the driver's seat. You have discovered a powerful and enjoyable means of motivating your dog and modifying its behavior to your liking.

Training must be effective. Training has to work, otherwise it's a bit of a waste of time—unless it's fun, of course. Fun training usually does work, though. Unpleasant training usually doesn't. When people try to train dogs by punishing them for inappropriate behavior, usually dogs don't learn what their people want them to learn. Instead, dogs learn those times when they can act like dogs without being punished. This German Shepherd learned that the best time to snack on garbage was when her person left the house to go out to dinner.

Easy

You know, saying "Whattt a good doggie," patting, stroking, scratching the little critter behind its ear, or even giving a food treat is all so effortless, while reprimanding or punishing a dog often requires considerable effort. One has to get up, get stern, and get over to the poor dog to deliver the punishment. Moreover, most punishment routines involve physical manhandling. Pushing, pulling, shaking, or "alpha-rolling" the dog can be quite tiring, and well beyond the physical capabilities of most novice dog owners. Considering that many dog-owning families include children (who try to mimic their parents' behavior), attempting to control a dog by physical punishment or force is not only cruel and stupid, it is potentially dangerous.

Phoenie says, "Training must be easy. Easy for people and easy for dogs. If training is not easy, the techniques may be well beyond the capabilities of many people, especially children. If training is not easy, some people may not even try. That's not good. Training must be easy."

Efficacious

Phoenie and Oso say, "Training must be efficacious.
Dogs don't want any unpleasant side-effects.

Dog training techniques must be effective, but they also must produce the desired effect without unwanted side-effects. Otherwise training could be counterproductive.

When reward-training goes awry, your dog may not completely master what you want it to learn, but it does learn to enjoy your ineffectual attempts at reward-training, and it does learn to develop a fondness for its hapless trainer—the reward-giver, i.e., you.

On the other hand, when punishment-training goes awry (as is often the case), your dog does not learn what you want it to learn. However, it does learn to dislike training, and to dislike its trainer, i.e., you. Punishment usually creates more problems than it resolves.

By definition, punishment decreases the frequency of immediately preceding behaviors. Apart from being de-motivating for the dog, repeated, ineffective punishment quickly erodes the very foundations of the relationship between dog and trainer. Also, technically, since ineffective punishment does not produce the desired effect of reducing unwanted behavior, the inflicted "nasties" may not accurately be defined as punishment. If punishment does not decrease unwanted behavior, then it is not punishment. It is merely harassment. Abuse—pure and simple abuse!

Enjoyable

Now, call me a worm if you like, but instead of having to play the bad guy, I would much rather praise my dog, pet her, and occasionally offer a tasty treat. And, as it happens, my dogs have all informed me that they much prefer my grateful, affectionate, and generous teaching-mode to any outdated, adversarial, and authoritarian approach. This means we are all happy.

So what have we got? User-friendly and dog-friendly dog training. I mean, if reading novels, watching television, eating chocolate, or playing golf were not enjoyable, we wouldn't engage in these behaviors, right? Similarly, if training is not utterly enjoyable, you're not going to do it either, are you? Well, I've got news for you: neither will your dog. So be sure to make training fun.

Oso says, "I'm logo-dog for the K9 Games
and a firm believer that training must be enjoyable.
If training isn't fun, many people won't bother with it,
and neither will many dogs. Training must be fun.

Pet dog training must be suitable for all family members (especially children) and for all pet dogs. Lure/reward techniques teach dogs to want to do what we want them to do. And the many rewards help build a strong relationship, as well as teaching dogs to like training and their trainers.

Jamie and Toby say, "Training must be expedient."

Expedient

Pet dog training techniques must be appropriate and suitable for all pet dog owners (men, women, and children) to train all types of pet dog—all breeds, all mixes, and all shapes and sizes.

Like most experts, dog trainers severely underestimate their own expertise and experience. Indeed, most dog training books describe complicated and time-consuming techniques, which the author (usually an adept and experienced trainer) uses to train specific breeds of dog (such as Golden Retrievers, Labrador Retrievers, Border Collies, German Shepherds, and Belgian Malinois), that have been selectively bred for their ease and excellence for competitive obedience, working trials, or protection work. Many of these methods and techniques are largely unsuitable for inexperienced trainers (most pet owners) and for many breeds and mixes of dog (especially quick little dogs, big cumbersome dogs, fearful dogs, and dogs with attitude).

1   Lure/reward training techniques are utterly expedient and entirely suitable for pet dog training.

2   Lure/reward training is the very best method for children to train pet dogs.

3   Lure/reward training offers the best techniques for teaching puppies basic manners.

4   Lure/reward training is the absolute method of choice for behavior modification, for socialization, and especially for temperament training, especially when working with fearful and aggressive dogs.

To summarize, lure/reward training offers the most suitable and appropriate choice of techniques for teaching any dog anything.

The owner-friendly and dog-friendly dog training techniques outlined in this little book are gentle, easy, efficient, effective, efficacious, expedient, and extremely enjoyable for you and you dog. And so without further ado, turn to Chapter 4, "Good Manners," and begin training your puppydog right away. Lure/reward training techniques work like a treat!

CHAPTER THREE
Food Lures and Rewards

So what do we normally use to lure dogs to show them what we want them to do, and what do we use to reward dogs for complying with our wishes? Food, glorious food—a tiny, tasty, delicious morsel of food.

And why do we use food? No, not because a dog food company has not offered me a palm-studded island in the Caribbean. If you followed my earlier recommendation to turn to the Good Manners section and get started with your dog right away, you already know the answer. Because it works. And, it works quickly. Food works so well, in fact, that I was able to take on the big four unpredictables— puppies, children, camera crews, and English weather—and still manage to film a television series without altogether making a fool of myself.

Food lures and rewards are used in the early stages of training to teach puppies and dogs *what* we want them to do, and to encourage them to *want* to do what we want them to do.

To teach puppies what we require of them, we pair each verbal request with a specific food lure movement (hand signal). Once the puppy learns the meaning of each verbal request or hand signal, food lures are no longer necessary and are phased out completely after just six to ten repetitions of any exercise. In a sense, the newly-learned verbal requests and hand signals may be used as effective lures to get the dog to do what we wish.

Food rewards are particularly effective early in training and in non-distracting settings. Using food rewards enables people and puppies to make a brilliant start to training and achieve enormous successes immediately. Nonetheless, food rewards are progressively phased out from the outset—after the very first correct response—by requesting the puppy to do more and more for each reward. As training progresses, food rewards are replaced with more meaningful incentives, such as praise, affection, toys, games, and activities. Eventually, no rewards are necessary; your dog does what you want because that's what it wants to do. In a sense, each response becomes its own reward. This is no different from children learning to speak, walk, read, dance, ski, or play golf. Performing each activity is more than sufficient reward as each behavior has become self-reinforcing.

Food lures and rewards work their magic in many aspects of a puppydog's education, especially during obedience training, behavior modification, and most especially temperament training—that is, when building confidence with fearful or aggressive dogs.

Food Rewards for Teaching Manners

Few people say "thank you" with feeling and meaning. Few people adequately thank others for cooking dinner, fetching them in the car, or putting out the garbage. And few people adequately thank their dog for a good job well done—for peeing and pooping in its doggy toilet, chewing its chewtoys, coming when called, and settling down quietly.

Many people are far too self-involved or self-conscious to engage in the sort of joyful, rapturous display of thanks that is meaningful to a puppy. Some people could barely bring forth praise suitable for a sick lettuce or partially-full tray of gravel. However, even the most inhibited or preoccupied of owners finds it simple to master the glorious art of offering a food reward. And the dog thinks that praise like that is just marvelous. A food reward is just our way of saying thank you to the dog for doing what we want. But this is not the only reason we use food in training.

Food Lures for Teaching Manners

Food is magically effective when used as a training lure. Most puppydogs would gladly oblige us and do what we want, if only they knew what we wanted them to do. Using lures is the absolute quickest way to teach dogs the meaning of our instructions. In a sense, much of training comprises teaching our dogs ESL (English as a Second Language): teaching dogs our words for their behaviors and actions.

Train your dog right...

...and she will...

...beg for more!

Squeaky toys, tennis balls, chewtoys, Frisbees, and snapping fingers may also be used, but food is the most effective lure for most dogs, and the most expedient lure for most novice trainers.

By using a food lure, it is easily possible to teach your dog to come, sit, and lie down in just a matter of minutes, without even touching your dog. Food lures may be similarly used to train dogs to follow and heel, to come and go just about anywhere (go inside/outside, go upstairs/downstairs, get in the back/front seat of the car, get in/out of the crate or kennel, get on/off the couch or bed), and to assume virtually any body position, e.g., sit, down, stand, roll over, beg, bow, back up, turn around, jump, etc.

Food Rewards for Behavior Modification

Behavior problems are the most common reason dissatisfied owners get rid of their dogs. In fact, simple housesoiling or destructive chewing are the most common terminal illnesses for domestic dogs. Dogs who repeatedly foul indoors or destroy household furniture are often surrendered to an animal shelter to play the lotto of life. Why? Simply because the owners failed to teach their dogs to use domestic toilets and toys.

Food rewards are extremely effective for motivating dogs to eliminate on command, to continue chewing appropriate chewtoys (stuffed with food), and to shush when requested.

Behavior modification can be difficult and time-consuming. By using food lures, changing behavior and creating good habits becomes quick and easy. Keep a screw-top jar of treats handy to your pup's toilet area and your pup will hurry to eliminate in that spot. Stuff chewtoys with your pup's dinner kibble and your pup will soon develop a chewtoy habit. Say, "Shush" and waggle a treat in front of your barking pup's nose and it will soon learn to shush on request. (Your pup cannot bark and sniff at the same time!)

Owners get very frustrated, and animated, when their dogs make a mistake, or a mess, or do something wrong. However, few owners are as expressive when it comes to praising their dogs for doing something right. If owners have a hard time praising their dogs for coming when called, can you imagine the level of "praise" for poor old Spot when he relieves himself at the right time in the right spot? "About time! Inside damn Spot!" What sort of reward is that?

Luckily, using food as a reward makes housetraining easy. In fact food rewards make all behavior modification easy—so very, very easy. The food reward adequately communicates your pleasure and approval, even if you can't. Now at least your dog knows what you're on about.

Food Lures for Behavior Modification

Food is an extremely effective lure for teaching dogs to stop barking on request, to dig only in its digging pit, and to chew nothing but chewtoys, i.e., to redirect normal, natural, and necessary doggy activities to outlets which people consider appropriate and acceptable for domestic living. Food lures enable you to mold and modify your dog's basic animal nature to your liking.

35

Food for Temperament Training

Food lures and rewards are flashy in obedience training and extremely effective for the prevention and treatment of behavior problems but if ever there were a mandatory use for food lures and rewards in training, it is for socializing dogs with people. Dogs that like people aren't scared and don't bite. And that's what dog-friendly dog training is all about.

We have to get puppies socialized. But it is not always advisable for strangers to praise or pet fearful or standoffish puppies or dogs. Although the puppydog may love being praised and petted by its owner, it may not necessarily enjoy being touched by unfamiliar people, nor may it relish the sound of their voices. In fact, the mere proximity of unfamiliar people, let alone their actions, may make a shy dog feel uneasy. Luckily, socialization becomes virtually effortless and enjoyable when using food lures and rewards. The dog may be gently enticed (lured) to approach an unfamiliar person and the dog is pleasantly surprised when the person offers a tasty food reward. And so the dog learns, "I like this person's presence, and I like this person's presents. People are good news!"

"My name is Ashby and I was a biter! Food lures and rewards saved my life. I first met Ian when I was confined outdoors to a drafty concrete passageway, where I had been protecting my dead master's shoe for six weeks. Ian offered a treat through the chain-link fence. I didn't trust him (because people hit me), so I bit Ian. But then he offered me another treat and took me home to live with Phoenix. He cooked me dinner—roast lamb with veggies. People gave me lots of treats. I learned to trust, and I didn't want to bite people anymore. I also learned to walk nicely on-leash, where to pee and poop, what to chew, and to howl and shush on request."

Food Critics

"Use food in training? That's sissy training"

Maybe so, but it works! And I'll tell you what, if carrying a wand and wearing a pink tutu would help train dogs and save their lives, I'd do that, too. Yes, food treats work a treat. In addition to their obvious applications in all aspects of teaching manners, food lures and food rewards may be more importantly used for behavior modification and temperament training. In fact, food lures and rewards are so effective, their use should be mandatory.

Ironically, though, throughout most of the last century, using food lures and rewards to train dogs and horses was considered to be unacceptable. Instead, force, punishment, harassment, humiliation, and abuse were the accepted "techniques" of the Trainers from The Dark Side! In fact to this day, there are still a few trainers who refuse to use food lures and rewards.

Perhaps these trainers are simply unaware of an entire century of scientific research and the consequential evolution of modern-day, psychological training techniques. Or perhaps these trainers are simply resistant, or scared, to adopt anything new, progressive, or more sophisticated.

Personally, I think most supposed criticism of food lures and rewards is merely a financial ploy. Food lure/reward training is just so incredibly efficient and effective that most dogs are well-trained within minutes. By advocating more time-consuming and laborious techniques, the trainer is able to keep clients for longer and extract more money!

Regardless of the fears of the unenlightened minority, it would be a shame if your puppy's education were to suffer simply because you had misgivings about using food lures and rewards. Consequently, here follow answers to other common concerns about using food in training.

"My dog will get fat!"

If you feed your dog too much, it will get fat. However, training treats should not be extra calories, and they should not be junk food. Food lures and rewards are part of your dog's normal daily diet (primarily consisting of dry kibble) but used periodically during training rather than given all at once at dinner time.

Each morning, measure out your dog's daily ration of kibble and put it in a handy container. (If your dog puts on weight, measure out less kibble each day and exercise your dog more. If your dog loses weight, measure out more kibble each day.) Throughout each day, use some kibble as lures and rewards for training, and stuff the remainder in hollow chewtoys.

A small number of treats (e.g., dog biscuits, or freeze-dried liver) may be included as part of your dog's daily dietary allotment of calories and these are best reserved for specialized training exercises, such as housetraining, park recalls, and socialization with children, men, and strangers.

"My dog will be forever on the scrounge, begging for food, and worrying at food in my hand!"
Not necessarily correct! You may use food distractions and rewards to teach the dog not to scrounge or worry at food in your hand. (See section on teaching "Off".) In fact, the only way to teach dogs not to scrounge or worry at food in your hand is by using food in training. In addition, you may teach your dog to take food (from your hand or dog bowl) only after being given a specific instruction, such as "Take It" or "Chow." The dog must learn the difference between children's hot dogs and doggy treats.

"Food makes my dog over-excited."
If food over-excites your dog, you need to use food as a reward to teach your dog to be calm. The DoggiCalm training technique is quick and easy. Let your dog sniff a piece of kibble in your hand, ignore the dog's boisterous bouncing and barking, wait for your dog to sit and then offer the kibble. Repeat the procedure a number of times. Delay giving the food reward for a couple of seconds after your dog sits and your dog will remain calm for a couple of seconds. With each successive repetition, progressively increase the delay and hence the period of calmness. After hand feeding just a dozen pieces of kibble, you'll have a dog that calms down quickly and sits automatically whenever you have food in your hand.

"It's demeaning to use food treats."
I have it from the highest authority that dogs strongly disagree with the above statement. On the contrary, dogs consider not receiving food rewards for their efforts to be demeaning.

I get paid when I write doggy books and give veterinary seminars. Most of you get paid when you work. And strange though it may seem, puppies and dogs would like to be on the payroll as well.

"My dog responds only when I have food."
Most probably because you have yet to fully grasp the principles of lure/reward training. Read on. Learn how to replace food lures with verbal commands and hand signals within your first training session, and learn how to phase out and replace food rewards with more meaningful incentives, such as life rewards and internal motivation.

"I don't want to bribe my dog."
Neither do I. Bribing is largely ineffective. Using food as lures, rewards, and general motivators is far more precise and effective than using food as bribes. Parents and politicians quickly learn that bribery does not work. Luring, rewarding, and motivating do work, extremely well, in fact. Lures teach dogs *what* we want them to do; rewards teach dogs to *want* to do what we want them to do; and motivators teach dogs to be eager and attentive *on cue*.

"I want my dog to respect me."
The above statement camouflages some pretty scary logic—that a dog would respect you more if you trained using correction and punishment, rather than lures and rewards. Duh!?! Beware the Trainers from The Dark Side, who insist that harassment, bullying, and physical domination are necessary to get dogs to show respect. Dogs' brains boggle at this perverse notion. On the contrary, you will gradually earn your dog's trust and respect with understanding, compassion, and intelligent education via lure/reward training.

We all want dogs to respect and be proud of their human companions. And especially we would like dogs to respect the wishes and feelings of children. Lure/reward training is absolutely the most expedient way for children to gain the respect of their dogs.

Consider for example, a child who takes five minutes to lure/reward train a dog to happily and willingly come, sit, and lie down off-leash. The child requests the dog to respond, and the dog respects the child's instructions and gladly obliges. Or put another way, the child commands the dog, and the dog complies. Most important though, the dog complies happily and willingly. And when it comes to children and dogs, willing compliance is the only way.

"I want my dog to do it for me!"
I want my dog to *want* to do it for me. I want dogs to voluntarily follow instructions because they have learned it is in their best interests to do so. Indeed, prompt and willing compliance are the cornerstones of dog-friendly dog training. Certainly it may be possible to coerce, or force, a dog to do things the trainer's way, especially if the dog is on leash and physically and psychologically held captive by restraint and force. However, when off-leash and out of arm's reach, the dog might just ignore the trainer's commands, leaving the trainer to train by himself.

"My dog doesn't like food."
Since food lure/reward training is so amazingly easy, efficient, and effective, I would teach every dog to like food, before commencing training. Puppies may easily be taught to appreciate food, simply by hand-feeding individual pieces of kibble throughout the day, rather than all at once from a bowl at mealtimes.

Pros and Cons of Training Tools

Any criticism of using food as a training tool may be applied to the use of any training tool, including leash-corrections and praise.

Excessive praise, or correction, may over-excite your dog. Your dog may not respond when off-leash, or when you do not have praise in your heart. Your dog is hardly going to respect someone who frequently resorts to force and punishment. And, what if your dog doesn't like food, you say? Well, what if your dog doesn't like leash corrections? Since the Trainers from The Dark Side could barely stop themselves from restraining, forcing, correcting, and punishing dogs in the past, such woolly logic should not stop owners from using food lures and rewards in the present and future!

The use of any training tool has its advantages and disadvantages. Do not forgo the magical advantage of using food lures and rewards just because of one or two supposed disadvantages. Learn to overcome the minor disadvantages so that you may take full advantage of many beneficial effects of food lures and rewards.

Food is the very best lure for most dogs and for most owners. However, once you have become adept at food luring, you will be able to use chewtoys, squeaky toys, and snapping fingers to lure your dog. Pieces of kibble and the occasional freeze-dried liver treat are the most convenient and easy-to-use rewards for initial training but you need to change to more meaningful "life rewards" as soon as possible. Of course, if you have a warm heart, an expressive voice, and affectionate hands, praise and petting will be more than a sufficient thank-you for your puppy.

Rules for Training Tools

1. Phase out the use of training tools as soon as possible.
Do not become dependent upon the training tools you use. Training tools are meant to temporarily facilitate training, not to permanently reduce reliability. Phase out the use of training lures and rewards as soon as possible, otherwise your dog will only respond when you have them. Once your dog is trained, it will gladly oblige your wishes and then your temporary training tools will no longer be necessary. Training lures become unnecessary as soon as your puppy learns the meaning of your verbal requests and hand signals. You should be able to phase out training lures completely during the very first session. Similarly, training rewards are no longer necessary once they have been replaced with more meaningful incentives—life rewards, such as dinner time, couch time, tummy rubs, car rides, walks, playing fetch, etc. You may begin to phase out training rewards during the first session, by asking your puppy to progressively perform more and more for a single piece of kibble.

2. Use training tools that your dog finds pleasant and enjoyable.
Most people understand dog training to involve manipulating or
modifying a dog's natural behaviors. The most common approaches
include increasing the frequency of desirable behaviors (using
rewards), teaching a dog to perform desired behaviors on cue (using
lures and rewards), and decreasing the frequency of undesirable
behaviors (using a "time out"—removal of reward opportunity).
However, there is a great deal more to training than behavior
modification. During the process, your dog forms many positive and
negative associations about training and about the trainer. If you use
pleasant training tools (lures and rewards), your dog will learn to love
training and the trainer. However, if you use unpleasant training tools
(restraint, physical coercion, correction, and punishment), your dog
will learn to dislike training, and the trainer, i.e., you!

Punishing your dog in an attempt to decrease undesirable behavior
may have the unwanted side-effect of teaching your dog to dislike
training and to distrust you. A more productive approach would be to
follow unwanted behavior with a verbal no-reward marker (such as
"Unacceptable behavior!", "Leave!", or "Be Gone!") to signal a short
time out from your presence and the prospect of any rewards. After
just a minute or so, call your puppydog and make up: "Puppy, come
here. Sit. Lie down. Goooood Puppy!" In just a few repetitions, short-
term puppy banishment will become the most effective way to banish
unwanted behavior. However, your dog will still love you—more so,
in fact. During each time-out, your pup will yearn to resume normal
social interactions and training. Once time-out from training has
become the most effective way to punish your dog, you will have
achieved the Holy Grail of Dog Training.

Nearly every trained animal you see in films and on television has
been taught using food lures and rewards. Killer whales are trained
using fish. Grizzly bears are trained using marshmallows and soda
pop. Obviously, trainers "in-the-know" do not want killer whales and
grizzly bears forming negative associations with training, or with the
trainer! Let's not discriminate against the canine species. Isn't it long
overdue for our best friends to have equal opportunity with the rest of
the trained animal kingdom?

Phoenie and Oso say,
"Food lures and rewards
for dogs!
Food lures and rewards
for dogs!!
Food lures and rewards
for dogs!!!"

CHAPTER FOUR
Good Manners

All you need to train your puppy is the inclination, a few sparks in your brain, a couple of pieces of kibble in your hand, and...the puppy. So, enough said—let's get going. Ask your pup whether it is ready to proceed by moving a food lure up and down in front of its nose. If your puppy nods in agreement, you're off and running. If your pup does not follow the food lure with its nose, either delay training until the pup shows more interest, or use something more enticing, e.g., freeze-dried liver, a favorite chewtoy, or a squeaky toy.

Strive for a really brilliant performance, not just a lackluster attempt. Use a variety of rewards (like a slot machine), and let the value of each reward reflect the quality of your pup's responses. Praise your puppy only for above average responses. Give praise and a piece of kibble for good responses, give praise and freeze-dried liver for better responses, and save the very best rewards (jackpots)— maybe a game, or a snuggle on the couch—for the very best responses. By rewarding your pup differently according to the standard of its responses, you'll find your pup's performance will continue to improve from day to day.

For the following exercises:

1 Request your puppy to do something. Say "Joe Pup, Sit" for example. Only if your puppydog is called Joe Pup, of course. Otherwise, substitute your dog's name for the generic "Joe Pup" used here. For example, the dog in these photographs is not really called Joe Pup—that's just his *nom de plume*. His real name is Oso. Also, you may substitute any personalized word for any instruction, provided you stick to the same request for each response throughout training. For instance, you may wish to train your dog in Spanish: "Jose Perrocito, Sientate!"

2 Show your puppy what you would like it to do by moving a food lure to entice your pup into the desired body position.

3 Praise your pup and reward it with a piece of kibble, a toy, or a game when it assumes the desired position.

Sit

1   Say "Joe Pup, Sit."

2   Keeping the lure close to your puppy's nose, slowly move it upwards and backwards over the pup's muzzle towards its eyes. As your pup lifts its nose to follow the treat, it will sit down. (Do not lift your hand too high or your puppy will jump up.)

3   As soon as your puppy sits, say "Good little doggie!" and offer a piece of kibble as a reward.

Is This Magic?

No, just a basic principle of quadrupedal, doggy engineering. Try it out for yourself. Crouch like a dog with both your fingers and feet touching the floor. Now try to look directly upwards at a spot on the ceiling, without lifting your fingers off the ground. You'll find it's impossible without bending your knees, squatting down, and assuming "the coyote howling at the moon posture". It's the same with dogs. If they want to look up, they have to sit down.

Now before this enormous training feat goes to your head and makes you giddy with success, let's just pause a while to peruse the list (on the facing page) of the many things your dog cannot do while it is sitting. You see, it's really that simple. All you have to do is teach your puppy a single command—"Sit!"—and then all of these potential problems become non-problems. For example, sitting and jumping-up are mutually exclusive behaviors; your dog cannot perform both simultaneously. So, if you teach your puppy to sit when greeting people, it will not jump up. In fact, the principle of sitting to avoid doing something else is so simple and effective that many dogs will sit as a ploy to avoid coming when called, heeling, grooming, rectal-temperature-taking, and anal-gland-squeezing. Not a bad ploy, if you ask me. Perhaps we should learn from our dogs.

But what did Joe Pup actually learn? Have you taught your puppy to sit? Well, not really. Your puppy knew how to sit when it was only three or four weeks old. More specifically, you have taught your puppy to sit on request. We are not so much concerned if and when your puppy decides to sit of its own accord, but rather, that it sits when requested to do so.

Also, you have taught your pup to sit on request only when it was already standing. For your puppy to respond reliably, it must additionally be taught to sit when it is lying down, and to sit from any other body position and activity. Thus, when teaching just three basic body positions—sit, down and stand—the first step is to teach six separate changes of body position: to sit when standing and lying down; to lie down when sitting or standing; and to stand up when sitting or lying down.

David Letterdog's List
of Things a Dog Cannot Do
While Sitting

1 Jump up, lick, paw, bump, or goose family, friends, visitors, or strangers, especially including the young and the elderly.

2 Bolt out of the front door or car.

3 Run off in the park.

4 Chase cars, cats, chickens, children, bicyclists, skateboarders, horses, and other dogs.

5 Bully, bother, pester, or disturb people or other dogs.

6 Get underfoot, stepped on, or tripped over.

7 Mount other dogs, or be mounted by other dogs.

8 Slap a child in the face, or clear a coffee table of wine glasses with a waggy tail.

9 Fence-fight or scrap through the garden fence.

10 Pace back and forth, chase its tail, or self-energize by running around like a whirling dervish from window to couch, from couch to carpet, and from carpet to window, etc., while working itself into a feverish frenzy.

Down from Sit

1 Say "Joe Pup, Down."

2 Waggle the lure in front your pup's nose. Quickly lower it to the ground between the pup's forepaws and hold it there palm downwards. Wait for your pup to lie down. Be patient. Inching the lure away from the pup's forepaws may facilitate the process as your pup reaches forward with its nose. Alternatively, slowly move the lure towards your pup's chest to cause the pup's rear end to plop down.

3 When your puppy lies down, say "Good little doggie" and maybe offer a food reward if it lies down promptly.

Sit from Down

1 Say "Joe Pup, Sit."

2 Hold the lure (palm upwards) in front your pup's nose and then quickly raise the lure upwards and backwards over the pup's head. You may need to waggle the lure or clap your hands over your pup's head to energize it to sit up. If your pup has rolled over to recline on its back, take one step backwards, bend down, and pat the ground in front of its nose. When your pup rolls back into the Sphinx position in preparation to get up, step in quickly and lure it to sit.

3 When your pup resumes sitting, praise and maybe offer a food reward if it sat up quickly.

Stand from Sit

1 Say "Joe Pup, Stand."

2 Slowly move the lure parallel to the ground, forward and away from your pup's nose. As the puppy stands, lower the lure a little to get the pup to look down. (If the pup looks up, it will promptly sit again after standing.) Do not lower the lure too far, though; the pup might lie down.

3 Calmly praise and maybe reward the pup to reinforce solid stands. Gently and rhythmically pushing down on the pup's withers helps solidify the stand stay. The firmer you push, the more solid the stay.

Down from Stand

1 Say "Joe Pup, Down."

2 Quickly lower the lure all the way to the ground and hold it palm down between the pup's forepaws. This position change is the hardest (see alternative method on page 55), so hold your hand steady until the puppy lies down. Once the pup's elbows and sternum touch the ground and the pup assumes a playbow posture, moving the lure towards the puppy's chest prompts the rear end to plop down.

3 Praise and reward accordingly (bear in mind this exercise is the most difficult). "Goooood Puppy. Good down!"

Stand from Down

1 Say "Joe Pup, Stand."

2 Move the lure upwards and forwards in front of your pup's nose. Again, if the pup is out for the count, stepping back and tapping the treat on the ground usually re-energizes the pup.

3 Praise and reward the pup on those occasions it stands up promptly.

Alternative Down

1 It can be a bit tricky teaching Down from the Stand. A simple ploy is to lure your dog under a coffee table, or even under your leg. Say "Joe Pup, Down."

2 Waggle the lure to pique your pup's interest.

3 As your pup sniffs the lure, slowly move it away from its nose...

4 ... and your pup will lie down to crawl under your leg!

Roll Over

1 "Sit" and "Down" are both good control commands. "Stand" is useful for examining your dog—at least for examining its top, front, back, and sides. To examine your dog's belly, you may crawl under the dog and look up, use a mirror on the end of a stick, or simply teach "Roll Over." Say "Joe Pup, Roll Over."

2 Move the lure alongside the pup's muzzle, backwards towards its ear. (Teaching "Roll Over" is easier when the dog is lying on one hip with both hind legs out to one side. Reposition your pup if necessary.)

3 Continue moving the lure over the pup's shoulder blades, and the pup will begin to roll. You may wish to pause at this stage to teach the pup to lie calmly on its side. (This is a "Side Stay" for examination).

4 Continue moving the lure, and the pup will roll onto its back. Again, you may wish to pause here to teach the pup to do a "Dead Dog Down" (supine Down with belly up).

5 To teach a complete Roll Over, continue moving the lure in one fluid motion until your pup is back...

6 ...in a "Down Stay" once more. "Gooood Puppy!" Your veterinarian will be forever grateful if you teach your dog "Stand Stay," "Side Stay," and "Dead Dog Stay."

Position Change Sequence:

Sit-Down-Sit-Stand-Down-Stand

Quantum Leaps

You will make four quantum leaps in training as you phase out hand-held training lures, and eventually all training rewards. Phasing out food lures is a simple matter—just put them in your pocket to be used as rewards for above-average responses. Phasing out food rewards is similarly simple—just empty your pockets of food and use something else as a reward.

1. Phasing Out Food Lures

As your pup learns to watch the movement of your hand-held lure, your hand movements soon become effective hand signals. Hold your hand palm-upwards for the Sit signal, and palm-downwards for the Down signal. After a few repetitions, your puppy will begin to anticipate each hand lure signal on hearing the relevant verbal command. Thereafter, the verbal request becomes the equivalent of a verbal lure, since it successfully prompts the desired response. Training lures are no longer necessary to entice your puppy into each position because a hand signal or verbal request is sufficient.

Put the kibble in your pocket right now. Come on, all of it! Repeat the Sit-Down-Sit-Stand-Down-Stand sequence with empty hands. However, make sure to follow each eager verbal request with a sweeping—nay flourishing—hand signal, just as if you were holding a lure. At the end of the sequence, praise your pup and reward it with a piece of kibble from your pocket. See, you don't need a food lure in your hand to get your dog to respond. Failure was all in your mind, just as the food is now in your pocket.

This is the first quantum leap: Your puppy has learned that although you have no food in your hand, you can still magically materialize all sorts of goodies from your pocket. Now it's time to begin fading out food rewards.

2. Reducing Food Rewards

Go back and use food as a lure for a quick test to see how many puppy-pushups (alternating sits and downs) your pup will do before it gives up. Keep hold of that treat though. The longer your hold on to the lure, the quicker training will proceed. (In fact, that's how we teach stays and "Off!") Now you know how much your puppy is willing to work for the prospect of just one food reward. See which family members and friends can get the puppy to perform the most push-ups for a single food reward. By asking more for less, you have begun to gradually and progressively phase out food rewards in training.

Now repeat the Sit-Down-Sit-Stand-Down-Stand sequence with empty hands but with food rewards in your pocket. Do not be in a hurry to stuff food rewards into your pup's mouth. Instead, treat every food reward as if it were a gold medal. Only reward your pup immediately following extremely rapid, or especially stylish responses.

This is a second quantum leap: Your puppy has learned that although you have food rewards in your pocket, it may not get one every time it responds correctly.

3. Phasing Out Food Rewards

Now it is time to empty your pockets and replace food rewards with praise, petting, toys, games, favorite activities, and other luxurious life rewards.

This is the third quantum leap: Your puppy has learned that although you have no food rewards in your pocket, even better surprises may follow desired behavior.

4. Phasing Out External Rewards

Eventually, it is no longer necessary to reward your dog to reinforce desirable behaviors. Rewarding your dog is always an option and always a wonderful thing to do, but your dog's stellar behavior is no longer dependent on expected rewards. Instead, your dog complies with your requests because it wants to.

After this fourth quantum leap, external rewards are no longer necessary, since your puppy's good behaviors have become self-reinforcing. In a sense, each correct response becomes its own reward. Really, this is no different from people who enjoy reading, running, riding, playing games and sports, and dancing. Rewards are not necessary. Participation is its own reward.

Hand Signals

After following the lure movements of your hand, which holds a treat or toy as lure, your dog will soon learn that palm upwards means "Sit"...

...and palm downwards means "Down."

Don't forget to praise and reward your dog for each correct response.

Stay

Once your puppy changes body positions quickly and eagerly on request, delay rewarding your pup for a couple of seconds after each position change. Quietly praise your pup while it remains (stays) in the appropriate position. In fact, count out the seconds, "Good sit-stay one... good sit-stay two... good sit-stay three... etc." Start with easily attainable goals, so your puppy can succeed. For example, three seconds for a Mastiff puppy, and just one second for a

wriggly Labrador. And for toy breeds and terriers, the deal is easier yet—if you stay still for just a quarter of a second, frozen in time for a palpable moment—then you'll get a food reward. Next time try for half a second, then a full second, then two seconds, three, five, eight, ten, fifteen seconds, and in no time at all, your puppy's stays will be measured in minutes. By gradually increasing the delay before rewarding your puppy on each successive trial, you are progressively increasing the length of the stay and phasing out the need for rewards.

Have competitions within the family to see who can withhold the food reward for the longest time while the puppy stays in each position. Vary the order of three body positions and make up your own sequences. For example, starting with a sitting puppy, instruct it in the sequence Down-Stand-Down-Sit-Stand-Sit. It is important to vary the lengths of stay in each in each position.

So, What Has Joe Pup Really Learned?

Well, if Mum has been training the pup in the kitchen, the young whippersnapper has learned, "When in the kitchen with Mum and a morsel, sitting when requested is not a bad idea." This does not necessarily mean the pup will pay attention to Dad, nor to young Jamie (bless his heart). Neither does it necessarily mean the puppy will pay heed to Mother in the living room, garden, or park. Nor, for that matter, does it necessarily mean the little critter will *always* sit for Mum in the kitchen. Basically, you have taught your puppy, only that it is beneficial to sit in certain highly specific situations.

If you want your puppy to obey each family member in all settings and situations, then every member of the family must train the pup in every setting and situation. In order to teach your puppy to respond here, there, and everywhere, it needs to be trained here, there, and everywhere. The secret is to train your puppy little but often—at least fifty training sessions a day, but with only a couple of sessions lasting for more than a few seconds.

To increase the number of short training interludes, integrate training into your daily routine and lifestyle. For example, perform a body-position sequence plus stays each time the clock chimes, whenever there are advertisements on the television, or every time you open the fridge, make a cup of tea, turn a page in a book or finish an article in the newspaper.

In fact, if you train your pup every time you remember you have a young, developing canine brain in your midst, the number of sessions will easily exceed fifty a day without your having to deviate from your normal lifestyle.

Life Rewards

Puppies are easy to train. It is so easy to teach them what we want them to do. In fact, a young puppy will do just about anything you ask just for the sake of doing it. As the puppy collides with adolescence, however, it begins to ask world-shattering questions, such as "Why?"

Just because your puppy has learned what "Sit" means does not necessarily mean it will sit when you request it to do so.

Consequently, the most important ingredient of any educational program, whether for children, employees, husbands, or dogs, is teaching "Why comply?" You must teach the relevance of complying. Indeed, once you have taught your puppy the positive consequences of cooperating, it will eagerly want to comply!

Integrate training into your dog's daily routine and lifestyle. First make a list of all the things in life your puppy enjoys. Then institute a simple and effective rule: Nothing will be denied, nor withheld from the pup, but the puppy has to sit beforehand. It's just common canine courtesy, really. Nothing more than a puppy "please."

In no time at all, your pup will learn the relevance of complying with your wishes and will be only too willing, eager, and happy to oblige. Now your dog will *want* to do what you want it to do.

Basically, you need to convince your pup that he or she is the trainer and you are the pupil! Your puppy needs to believe, "Sitting is the canine cue—the veritable key to the door—which makes my owners do anything I want. If I sit, they will open doors (how courteous). If I sit, they will massage my ears (how affectionate). If I sit, they will share the couch (how cooperative). If I sit, they will throw the tennis ball (how athletic). And if I sit, they will serve supper (how well-trained)."

Make sure your dogs sit for their supper.

Ask Your Puppy to Sit

1   Before greeting people

2   Before greeting other dogs

3   Before coming inside

4   Before being allowed on the couch

5   Before cuddling on the couch

6   Before being put on leash

7   Before going outside

8   Before moving away from the front door

9   Before getting in the car

10   Before getting out of the car

11   Before being let off leash

12   Before you throw a tennis ball

13   Before you take the ball back

14   Before throwing the ball again

15   And yes, before your puppy gets its supper.

Aside from producing a more reliable dog, integrating training into the daily routine of your dog makes your life more enjoyable, and allows your dog to have more fun and freedom. For example, something as simple as going through a door with an untrained and uncontrollable dog can be a time-consuming and daunting prospect. It can take some owners almost five minutes to put on the leash and make their exit. This means leaving the house with the dog just once a day may easily waste more than a whole fortnight over the lifetime of the dog. That's the equivalent of fourteen entire days and nights spent struggling with dogs in doorways. The result, of course, is that many owners do not bother to walk the dog at all if it's that much trouble.

On the other hand, well-trained dogs get to be taken on walks, picnics, days out, and car trips with their owners, and they are far less likely to be relegated outdoors, or isolated in a back room when visitors arrive. A well-trained dog has much more fun.

Settle Down and Shush

Right from the outset, make frequent little quiet moments part of your dog's daily routine. Remember, a puppy is not like an irritating child's toy. You cannot simply remove the batteries from a rambunctious adolescent dog. Instead you must learn how to "turn off" your dog. Learn to use walks and your puppy's favorite and most exciting games as rewards for settling down quietly and calmly.

Throughout the course of the day, have your puppy settle down for longer periods at home. For example, when watching the television, have your pup lie down on-leash, or in its bed, but during the commercial breaks, release the puppy for short, active play-training sessions.

When playing with your puppy, have it settle down and shush every 30 seconds or so. To begin with, have the pup lie still for just two seconds before letting it play again. Use a release command, such as "Free Dog," "At Ease," or "Let's Play." After 30 seconds, interrupt the play session again with a three-second quiet moment. Then try for four seconds. And then five, eight, ten, and so on. Alternate "Settle Down" with "Free Dog" and with each repetition, it becomes progressively easier to get your puppy to settle down quickly.

Once your pup gets the picture, the exercise may be profitably practiced on walks. When walking round the block, periodically have your puppy settle down for just a few seconds before resuming the walk. An entertaining way to train is to instruct your pup to settle down every twenty yards or so, while you read an article from the newspaper, or a page from a good book, such as Jean Donaldson's doggy bestseller, *The Culture Clash.*

With the above exercises, your puppydog will learn to settle down quickly following a single command, no matter how excited or distracted it may be. Moreover, your dog settles down willingly and happily because it knows being told to lie down is not the end of the world, and not necessarily the end of the walk. Rather, your dog has learned, "Settle Down" is just a relaxing time-out for gentle praise and affection before its exciting life as Activity Dog resumes once more.

It is difficult to have too many rules with a young pup. Teach your puppy to be calm and controlled when requested. and there will be years of enjoyment ahead. Let your puppy pull on-leash, and it will pull on-leash as an adult. Let your puppy play indiscriminately and without frequent interruption, and it will become inattentive and uncontrollable as an adult. Integrate play and training, and integrate training and walks. In no time at all, training will be fun, and fun activities (play and walks) will be structured.

Integrate walks with frequent "Sits" and "Settle Downs."

"If I sit awhile, my owner will continue our walk."

Give your puppy a stuffed chewtoy to help it settle down quickly and quietly...

...so that you may enjoy reading another chapter from your book.

Recalls

Have somebody hold your puppy. Take a tasty treat in one hand and show it to the pup. Say "Look what Daddy has and you don't," and then move away from your pup. Call your pup: "Joe Pup, Come." Squat down, open your arms invitingly, and waggle the food lure in front of you. Praise your puppy all the time it heads in your direction. When your puppy reaches you, give it a huge hug (making sure to take the pup by the collar, just so you know you could if need be). Maybe offer the treat as a reward and then release the puppy and tell it "Go play."

Whenever your puppy is off-leash, investigating or playing in the yard or park, instruct it to come to you every couple of minutes or so.

1 With somebody holding your puppy, or with your puppy left in a sit stay, say "Joe Pup, Come."

2 Open your arms invitingly, waggle the food or toy lure in front of you, and praise your pup enthusiastically all the time it approaches. Remember, your puppy's first step towards you is the most important step to praise. Reward the puppy's first and subsequent steps towards you.

However, give your puppy a food reward only for one out of every two recalls. Obviously, reward your pup after the faster recalls. If you reward your puppy after every recall, it may not learn that you want it to come quickly. In this exercise we are using food as a lure to entice the pup to come, and as an occasional reward to reinforce the puppy for coming quickly. However, the real rewards are your praise and the words "Go Play." Say nothing after slower recalls. Simply repeat the process. After a few trials your puppy will come so fast that small breeds will be hard to catch, and large breeds will flatten you. Consequently, it is a smart preemptive plan to instruct your pup to sit when it is homing-in and only three or five puppy-lengths away from potential impact.

3   Once your puppy is within three to five dog-lengths, instruct your pup to "sit" and give the hand signal to sit with the right hand (palm upwards with food or toy lure enclosed).

4   Tell Joe Pup that you are overjoyed that he has successfully accomplished yet another wonderful and glorious recall. Maybe offer a food treat, or reward the pup with a game with its toy after especially zippy recalls, and then tell Joe Pup to "Go Play."

Walking On-Leash

Walking with your dog is one of the most enjoyable activities. Unfortunately, many dogs seem to enjoy pulling on leash. Bearing in mind that the dog weight-pulling record is well in excess of 10,000 pounds, it is not a good idea to allow your pup to develop a pulling habit. Leash-pulling often advertises a lack of control. If the leash were not present, neither would your dog. It is unfair to allow a puppy to pull on leash if later in life it will receive many reprimands for the very same activity. This is a drag for the dog, and a drag for the owner. Eventually, most owners decide not to walk leash-pullers at all because, sadly, walking has become a drag.

The best way to deal with leash-pulling is never to allow it to become a problem. Never continue walking with your puppy, not even for a single steplet, unless your puppy's leash remains loose, i.e., slack, lax, and floppy. This can be a difficult endeavor with a young puppy, let alone an adult dog. So on-leash walking is best accomplished via a progressive and systematic process:

1   Teach your puppy to follow you when off-leash so that it understands the notion of staying close and develops a psychological bungee cord.

2   Teach your puppy to heel (for closeness) and sit (for control) off-leash. Teaching your puppy to heel off-leash teaches you to pay attention to your puppy.

3   Teach your puppy to heel on-leash. This is easy. Just attach the leash and off you go.

4   Now, on-leash walking is a much easier prospect. However, if you are still experiencing difficulties, there are a number of techniques that will help: Red-Light/Green-Light, On-Leash Following, and Troubleshooting Problem Scenarios.

1. Following Off-Leash

Let your puppy off-leash only in safe areas, (e.g., indoors, in a fenced yard, or in a dog park). Walk away from your puppy and it will follow you. There are two simple rules to entice your puppy to follow:

1   Keep moving...

2   Away from your puppy.

This may sound simplistic, but try it. I guarantee, in the space of a few seconds, the average three-month-old pup can train an off-leash owner to slow down, walk backwards, pirouette, stand-stay, recall, and follow. Remember, the puppy cannot follow you unless you are going somewhere. And, unless you are moving away from the pup, you'll most certainly end up following it. That is not the aim of the game. The pup is meant to learn to follow you. And so, move off quickly, and keep moving away from your puppy at all times.

If your puppy tries to improvise when following, and starts to lag or heads off in an alternative direction, alert your pup to its transgression – "Oi! Come along," and dramatically accentuate your puppy's mistake by quickly zooming off in the opposite direction.

Your puppy will smartly self-correct as if on a bungee cord. If your puppy slows down, speed up. If your puppy rushes on ahead, slow down, or turn about and run back from where you came. If your pup drifts left, turn right, and if the pup wanders right, turn left and speed up. Praise your pup the instant it starts to catch up.

Your puppy will quickly learn that it cannot divert its attention from you for a single second without you heading off in some new direction. Consequently, your pup will begin to pay attention and follow. For puppies who are too young to be walked on the streets because they have not yet completed their course of immunizations, the following exercises are easily practiced in the house and garden. Get your puppy to follow you inside and outside, upstairs and downstairs, into different rooms, and around tables and couches. Preparatory private practice prevents predictable poor performance and problematic pulling predicaments in public places.

Regular, long, off-leash puppy walks (in safe areas) are the secret to calm and controlled on-leash walking. Your puppy needs to develop a centripetal attraction towards you. Your off-leash pup must always feels a gravity-pull towards the most important body in its universe—you. It is essential to develop off-leash owner-gravity before trying to walk your puppy on-leash. If your puppy doesn't walk close to you when off-leash, it will surely pull when on-leash.

Pulling is basically an advertisement that your dog does not want to walk by your side, and presumably would *not* walk by your side if it were not restrained by a leash. Either your puppy considers that investigating the environment is much more interesting than you, or your puppy simply does not enjoy walking by your side because you keep jerking the leash to try to dissuade it from pulling. (By moving ahead and tightening the leash, the puppy reduces the pain of each jerk.)

Owner-gravity (following) exercises are time-sensitive. It is not safe to walk your puppy on public property until it is at least three months old, and by the time the puppy is 18 weeks old, following exercises start to lose effectiveness. Untrained adolescents soon develop doggy interests and would much rather sniff urine and feces, sniff other dog's rear ends, or simply sniff, than walk by their owner's side. It is much easier to teach off-leash following and closeness before your puppy reaches adolescence.

Take long walks and keep moving away from your puppy. Accentuate your pup's unwanted wanderings by smartly moving off in the opposite direction. Should your puppy get too far ahead, hide. Periodically, shout your pup's name. Remain hiding but keep an eye on your pup. Wait for the puppy to find you and then lavish it with praise. It is unlikely that you will be able to hide from your pup more than a couple of times. Perhaps your puppy thinks that it cannot take its eyes of you for a second without you getting lost.

During each walk, remember to frequently instruct your pup to sit or settle down by your side. You can lure and reward your off-leash puppy to settle down beside you simply by holding a piece of rope with a stuffed chewtoy tied to the end.

2. Heeling Off-Leash

1   Practice off-leash heeling in a safe area (indoors, or in a fenced yard). Use a lure in your left hand to position the puppy on your left side when in motion, and transfer it to your right hand to signal the puppy to sit when you stop. (Or hold lures in both hands.) With your pup sitting on your left side, say "Joe Pup, Heel" and give a hand signal by moving the lure in your left hand from left to right in front of your dog's nose.

2   Walk briskly forward in a straight line, waggling the lure in your left hand and praising your pup as you go.

3   Transfer the lure from left to right hand in preparation for the sit signal.

4   Say "Joe Pup, Sit," and while in motion, give a sit signal in front of your pup's face with your right hand.

5   Then come to a halt and praise your puppy as soon as it sits: "Good Heel-Sit Joe Pup. Good Heel-Sit."

6   Well, since that was so good, how about a friendly pat of encouragement before proceeding on the next Sit-Heel-Sit sequence.

Teaching your puppy to heel with precision is the most complicated of all training exercises. To make the process as easy as possible, break down heeling into a series of simpler exercises.

1 Teach your puppy to sit quickly and reliably.

2 Teach your puppy to come and sit in heel position.

3 Teach left-, right-, and about-turns in place.

4 Teach straight-line, sit-heel-sit sequences.

5 Combine all the exercises and make turns while in motion.

Before heeling anywhere, make sure that your puppy sits reliably. If your puppy does not sit promptly when requested, you will become frustrated and quickly ruin your pup's desire to heel by repeatedly nagging at your puppy to sit after it heels well.

Teach your puppy precise heel position while stationary. Say, "Puppy, Heel," and use a lure in your right hand to lure your puppy to sit by your left side. Take one step in any direction (forwards, backwards, right, or left), or pivot in place (90°, 180°, 270°,

Use your left hand to guide your puppy while turning in place.

clockwise, or counter-clockwise), and then stand still, say, "Puppy, Heel," and lure your pup to come and sit in heel position again. Repeat this process over and over in a number of different distracting settings—in the house, the yard, and the dog park.

Practice heeling turns in place. Instruct your puppy to sit and then pivot on the spot, using your left-hand food lure to guide your dog around, and your right-hand lure to get your puppy to sit again, facing in the new direction—sit-turn-sit. Practice turning clockwise and counter-clockwise.

Each heeling sequence begins and ends with the dog sitting by your left side. To keep your pup in heel position when in motion requires continual attention and repeated enthusiastic feed-back. Consequently, think of heeling as short sit-heel-sit sequences. Each sit allows you to catch your breath and regain composure.

Make sure you always start each sequence with the pup in the correct position—sitting on your left side. Use the lure in your right hand to position the pup by your left side. Say "Joe Pup, Sit," and give a hand signal by moving your right hand across your body— upwards and backwards in front of the dog's nose. Transfer the lure to your left hand in preparation for heeling.

1   Establish your composure with your pup sitting in heel position.

2   Heel rapidly in a straight line for a very short distance.

3   Have your pup sit again to re-establish your composure.

For turbo-pups, maybe start with single-step sequences. Your pup will pay much more attention after a series of short, staccato sit-step-sit sequences. Now try for two steps between sits. Then try three, five, eight, and ten steps at a time. Repeat the short heeling sequences, gradually increasing the number of steps between sits. Soon you will be doing long straightaway heels.

Initially, walk as quickly as possible so that your puppy has to walk a straight line in order to keep up. If you amble along, your puppy will have ample opportunity to serpentine from side to side.

Initially, heel only in a straight line. Keep your puppy's attention by frequently changing pace. Say "Quickly" before speeding up, and say "Steady" before slowing down. Your pup will quickly learn the meaning of these two very useful instructions.

Remember to make it fun. Praise your puppy frequently, and occasionally dispense a food reward after an exceptionally good bit of heeling, or after a stylish, or lickety-split sit.

When you are ready to turn, instruct your puppy to sit, and then turn in place—sit-turn-sit. Then heel away in a straight line in the new direction. After no time, you will be able to begin negotiating turns while moving.

Moving Right Turns

1 To avoid your dog taking a shortcut behind you on right turns, say "Quickly!"

2 Move your left hand forwards to speed up your pup so that its head is in front of your left knee before you turn right. Speed up to encourage your puppy to complete the turn quickly.

3 After the right or right-about turn praise the puppy when it comes back into heel position.

Moving Left Turns

1 To avoid bumping your puppy when making left turns, say "Steady!"

2 Slow down and move your left hand behind your left knee to slow down the pup.

3 After the left or left-about turn, praise the puppy when it comes back into heel position.

3. Heeling On-Leash

1 Before walking your puppy on-leash, teach it to heel on-leash. You will pay much more attention to the tension in the leash when heeling rather than walking. To keep your dog motivated, use lots of praise and rewards.

2 To keep your dog attentive, change speeds often, and frequently instruct and signal your dog to sit. Your dog will soon learn to watch you and to watch your hand signals.

3 Praise your dog while it remains in variable length sit-stays at heel position.

4. Walking On-Leash

Red-Light/Green-Light

1   Stand still with your puppy on-leash. Hold the leash in both hands held close to your chest. Do not move. Eventually—it may take a few minutes (or several minutes)—your puppy will stop pulling. In fact, once your pup realizes that it is going nowhere, your pup will probably sit or lie down. Not bad, eh? You get free sits and downs in this exercise.

2.   Praise your puppy and offer a food reward as soon as it sits (or lies down) with a slack leash, say "Let's go," and then take a single large stride.

3   Stand still once more and wait for your puppy to sit again. Be prepared to take the strain when you stop. Your single step will energize the pup, causing it to lunge forward like a Dog-on-Duracell (aptly demonstrating the colossal reinforcing properties of being allowed to pull on leash). Hold your ground until your puppy sits down, then take another single step and stand still.

After a few repetitions your pup will walk forward calmly, knowing there is little point in hurrying ahead because you never seem to go farther than one step. Also, your puppy will sit promptly when you stop because it has learned that while lunging makes you stop (red light), sitting makes you go (green light).

Once you can alternate single steps and standing still, try taking two steps before standing still. Then take three steps and stand still. Then five, then eight, and then twenty steps before stopping. Before you know it, your puppy will walk calmly and attentively by your side on a loose leash, and whenever you stop, your puppy will automatically sit promptly and attentively (in anticipation of you stepping forward one more).

On-Leash Following

An alternative leash-walking approach is to hold the leash in both hands held close to the front of your body and to start walking at a steady pace and not stopping. Do not jerk the leash. As with the following exercise described earlier, whenever your puppy pulls in any direction, simply turn in the opposite direction and gently walk away at the same steady pace. If your pup pulls ahead, about-turn and smoothly walk the other way. Your puppy will learn surprisingly quickly to walk calmly by your side.

Troubleshooting Problem Scenarios

If your puppy pulls on leash only at certain times, practice in those specific situations.

For instance, if your pup pulls when leaving home, practice leaving home. Put your pup on leash, walk out of the front door, about turn, go back inside, and take your puppy off leash. Then start again and repeat the entire sequence half a dozen times in a row. Characteristically, the first try may assume epic proportions. The second exit is a little easier. The third is easier still and by the sixth time you leave the house, your puppy is next to perfect. Your pup has become as bored as you are with the exercise, so it no longer charges off with the excited anticipation of a walk. Instead, once your pup leaves the house calmly, it gets to go on a walk. Now the walk becomes a reward for mannerly behavior, rather than a reward for unruly behavior.

If your puppy pulls more vigorously during the initial part of the walk and is calmer coming home, take your puppy on a series of short identical walks rather than one long exciting one. Leave the house (as described above), walk round the block, come back home, and take your puppy off-leash. Then repeat the process. You will find with successive laps, your puppy becomes calmer, less distracted, and progressively more manageable each time it sets off.

If your puppy pulls when approaching the dog park, practice entering the dog park in a mannerly fashion. Slowly approach the dog park and whenever the puppy pulls, turn around, walk away from the park for a few steps, stop and wait for the puppy to sit, and then turn around and walk slowly towards the park again. Repeat this until it is possible to enter the park without your puppy pulling. Let the puppy play for a while to let off steam and then call the puppy, put it on leash, leave the park, and then re-enter. Leave and re-enter the park a number of times during a single visit. You'll find your puppy's manners improve each time you re-enter the park.

If your puppy pulls while approaching another dog, practice approaching other dogs. Engage a friend to sit on a park bench with their dog on-leash. Slowly approach the other dog, and whenever the puppy pulls, turn around, walk away from the dog for a few steps, stop and wait for the puppy to sit, and then turn around and walk slowly towards the dog again. Repeat this until it is possible to walk up to the other dog without your puppy pulling. Make sure you stop and wait for your puppy to sit before allowing it to greet and sniff the other dog. Then repeat the process: walk your puppy away from the dog and then turn around and let it walk up, sit, and greet the other dog again. You'll find walking on-leash gets easier and easier with each repeated greeting.

If your puppy pulls on a particular section of the sidewalk (e.g., past a particular house, or schoolyard), practice walking back and forth on that section of the sidewalk until your puppy is picture perfect.

Face up to your problems and solve them when they occur. It's so much easier in the long run. Then you and your faithful companion can enjoy long walks together for a long time to come.

Walking the Dog...

Ask your puppy to sit before opening any door or gate, and soon it will do so automatically.

Calm your pup when walking on-leash by integrating many sits into the walk. Ask your puppy to sit at least every twenty yards or so.

Remember that the good old dog walk is the highest reward in domestic dogdom. Each time you stop the walk and instruct your puppy to sit, you may reward your pup for sitting by resuming the walk.

...and Taking Time to Enjoy the Moment

Integrate many settle-downs into your puppy's walk. The longer your pup settles down, the calmer it will be when you resume walking on-leash once more.

Occasionally, offer your puppy a chewtoy stuffed with kibble and treats to lure it to settle down for a good chew, while you settle down for a good read.

And sometimes, just take the time to enjoy the moment with your dog. You know, those that we grieve tomorrow are alive and well today. Take the time to enjoy your dog. Take the time to savor life.

CHAPTER FIVE
Socialization

Socialization is the second most important consideration for any companion dog. (Teaching bite inhibition is the *most* important concern for any domestic animal.) Although it is possible to live with an unruly dog with a variety of bad habits, it is not much fun living with a dog who does not like people—particularly if the dog doesn't like you. Always treat your pup kindly and establish a firm foundation of mutual trust and understanding. Make a point of introducing the puppy to a wide variety of people.

Do not be duped by the fact that your puppy acts fine with you. Certainly, the first step in socialization is to make sure your puppy is perfectly friendly with family, friends, and neighbors. However, it is also imperative that your dog becomes Mr. Sociable around strangers so that the dog does not object when examined by the veterinarian, or when playfully hugged by a child in the park. On the whole, dogs tend to feel very uneasy around children, men, and strangers. Put the three together and what have your got? Unfamiliar little boys!

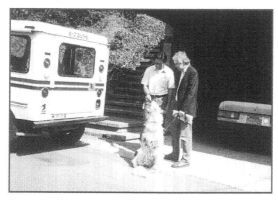

Meeting our mailman on one of our daily walks, I convinced him to give Phoenix a piece of kibble for sitting. The more people you can enlist to help train your puppy, the easier it becomes.

Also, do not be duped by the fact your *puppy* is fine with people. All puppies should be fine with people. The concern is whether your puppy will grow up into an adult dog who still likes people. Your pup will go through a lot of changes on the road through adolescence. A major change occurs between five and eight months of age when developing adolescent dogs become increasingly wary of unfamiliar people and situations. Make sure your puppy has ample opportunity to become familiar and friendly toward a wide variety of people.

Your goal during early puppyhood is to super-socialize your puppy. Create a puppy who loves all types of people and enjoys every conceivable situation. Your puppy must have bags and bags of confidence in preparation to negotiate the stressful months of adolescence. Doggy antipathy towards children, men, and strangers is likely if your puppy does not have sufficient contact with people, or if your puppy's social contact is frightening or unpleasant.

For the time being, start inviting people to your house to meet, hand-feed, and lure/reward-train your puppy. Invite people in droves. Invite family, friends, neighbors, and work colleagues. Ask everyone to bring extra friends. Invite men, women, and children. During your puppy's first four weeks at home, you simply cannot introduce it to too many people.

When your puppy is three months old, take it everywhere with you. Take it for car rides, on errands, to the bank, and to shopping centers. Walk that puppy! And especially take time on your walks to sit down, relax, and allow your pup plenty of opportunity to watch the world go by.

First Impressions

Initial greetings generally leave an indelible impression, so you must actively make sure the puppy's first meetings with people are pleasant, enjoyable, and controlled. Make sure you carry kibble to give to any visitor or passerby who wishes to say hello to your pup. Insist that everybody lure/reward your puppy to sit before petting it. Make no exception and in no time at all, your puppy will learn to sit automatically in anticipation of greeting people.

Family First

Starting with the family, everyone should introduce themselves to the puppy by offering a treat, then backing up and enticing the puppy to approach and sit for a second treat. Repeat this sequence for a third and maybe a fourth treat. We call this routine "The Casablanca Treatment"—"This could be the beginning of a beautiful friendship." By offering treats, we are letting the pup know we want to be friendly. By approaching and sitting close, the puppy demonstrates sociability and compliance—happy, friendly compliance. And when we consider the dog's attitude towards children, friendly compliance is the only way to go.

Handling and Gentling

Regularly cradle, cuddle, and hug your puppy so it becomes like putty in your hands. Massage, handle, and examine every part of its body. Examine its muzzle, mouth, teeth, both ears, and all four paws. Feed your puppy dinner kibble as you do so. Make sure you instruct family and friends (especially children) to do the same, and then your dog will enjoy being hugged by children and handled and examined by the veterinarian.

As early as possible, get your puppy used to being picked up, cradled, and hugged. Carefully lay your pup on its side and on its back. Gently massage your pup's chest and belly to soothe and mesmerize the little critter. Handle every part of the pup, especially its ears, muzzle, collar, paws, and rear end. Hand-feed the pup while you are handling it. Your puppy will quickly realize it is on to a good thing. Gently brush the puppy and flea-comb it. Especially introduce your pup to the nail clippers. In fact, "Casablanca" the nail clippers. "Yo Pup! Look here…nail clippers! And…heeeeere's a treat." Touch your pup's paw with the clippers and give it another treat. Then hold the paw and offer a treat from the hand containing the clippers. Pretend to clip a puppy nail, give a treat, and then put the clippers away. That's enough for today. Your dog will say, "Waahhh! I want my nails clipped again!" Next time, actually clip the nails on one paw and offer a treat. "I've got three more paws, you know." Get your puppy used to new things gradually, and it will quickly learn to enjoy them.

Hand-Feeding

Do not get into the bad habit of putting down your puppy's food bowl and then walking away. If you do, your puppy will become accustomed to eating alone and it may grow to resent company around its food bowl as it approaches adolescence. Instead, spend time with your pup while it is eating. Make a point of hand-feeding. If you hand-feed tastier, freeze-dried liver treats while your puppy is eating regular kibble from its food bowl, it will soon learn to welcome company at dinner time.

Have the family sit around and hold the puppy's bowl. While it is eating dry kibble, occasionally spoon in scrumptious canned food. Or, have someone dip a hand in the puppy's kibble to reveal a really tasty freeze-dried liver treat. After a few repetitions perhaps the dog muses, "It sure beats me how on earth they keep finding yummy treats in my bowl. I could have sworn that my nose-scan diagnosed a treat-free bowl. Boy! I sure like these people around my dinner bowl, and I just love it when they dip their hands in!"

During each meal, take away the puppy's bowl of dry kibble to add a dollop of juicy, canned food before replacing the bowl. "Ah!" thinks the dog. "So that's why they wanted the bowl, they'd forgotten the dessert!" These exercises will go a long way to prevent any possessiveness over food later in life. This is a vital safety precaution, particularly if you have children in the family.

It is not sufficient for your dog to tolerate people's proximity and actions around its food bowl. Your dog must *thoroughly enjoy* company while eating.

"Phoenix, Off!"

"Phoenix, Take it.

Off and Take It

Weigh out your puppy's daily diet of kibble in the morning, feed small portions in a bowl at mealtimes, and then hand-feed the rest throughout the day. You can teach your puppy the meaning of "Off," "Take It," and "Gently" during hand feeding exercises.

Hold a piece of kibble firmly in your fingers, and this is the deal: "If you don't touch this food treat for just one second after I softly say 'Off,' I will say 'Take It' and you can have it." In fact, offer the first treat the instant your pup withdraws his nose and breaks contact with your hand. Once your pup has mastered this simple task, up the ante to two seconds of non-contact, and then three, five, eight, twelve, twenty and so on, before saying "Take It" and offering the kibble. Count out the seconds and praise your dog for each second of non-

Young puppies have no bite inhibition, and they bite hard and often. However, although puppy teeth are needle sharp, their jaws are relatively weak, and so puppy bites seldom cause injury. Learning bite inhibition is the most important item on every puppy's educational agenda. First puppies must learn to inhibit the frequency of their bites, and then the force of their bites. Once established, bite inhibition progressively worsens as dogs grow older. Regular hand-feeding is the best way to maintain bite inhibition

contact: "Good dog one, good dog two, good dog three..." and so forth. If your puppy touches the kibble or your hand before being told to take it, simply repeat "Off!" and start the count from zero again. Your pup will learn that it cannot have the kibble until it has not touched it for say, eight seconds, and until you say "Take It." It also learns, the quickest way to get the kibble is not to touch it for the first eight seconds when instructed "Off."

"Off" has many useful applications: To instruct your puppy to stop mouthing; leave the cat alone; ignore the cat's litter box; not touch people-food on the table; not touch the table, the baby, a fearful dog, an aggressive dog, a decayed crow, a fecal deposit of unknown denomination, etc., *ad nauseum.*

Also, your puppy learns to take objects on request. This will help later in retrieval training. So let's have a new house rule. Your puppy is never allowed to take food, or any object, from any person's hand, unless instructed to "Take It."

"Off" and "Take It" allow you to prepare and serve your dogs' dinner in a mannerly fashion. (Above)

"Off" and "Sit" allow you to eat your dinner in peace. (Right)

95

Gently

Regular hand feeding helps create and preserve a soft mouth in your dog. If ever the puppy lunges or snaps at the food, say "Ouch!" whether it hurt or not. Shouting is not necessary, but do take a five-second time-out from hand-feeding while you pretend to lick your wounds, and then say "Gennnnntly" in a soft voice and offer the food again. You are reproducing the sort of response the pup would expect from its mother or littermates if it had behaved too roughly. All contact would be suspended until the pup calmed down and approached again with more care and consideration.

Controlling Puppy Biting

Puppies bite! And thank goodness they do. Play biting is a normal, natural, and absolutely necessary facet of puppy development. A pup that does not mouth and bite much as a youngster augurs ill for the future. Play-biting is the means by which puppies develop bite-inhibition. The combination of weak jaws, needle-sharp teeth, and the puppy's penchant for biting results in numerous painful play-bites.

Teaching your puppy to inhibit the force and then the frequency of its bites, and to develop a soft mouth, is by far the most important aspect of puppy husbandry.

Although some puppy bites may be quite painful, they seldom cause serious harm. However, occasional painful puppy bites plus your appropriate feedback are absolutely essential for your puppy to develop reliable bite-inhibition and a soft mouth. Moreover, it is essential that your maturing pup receives repeated feedback regarding the force of its bites before it develops jaws strong enough to cause real damage.

So beware of the temptation to punish your pup in an attempt to get it to stop play-biting altogether. At best, your puppy will avoid mouthing those family members who can punish it effectively, and instead direct its mouthing sprees towards those who cannot, i.e., children. At worst, your puppy will stop play-biting altogether, and hence will not develop bite inhibition.

The reliability of your puppy's bite-inhibition as an adult directly depends upon adequate puppyhood opportunities to play-bite people, other dogs, and other animals. The more your puppy play-bites, the safer will be its jaws and the better its bite inhibition as an adult.

For puppies that do not grow up with the benefit of regular and frequent interaction with other dogs and animals, the responsibility of teaching bite inhibition lies entirely with their owners, i.e., you, your family, and friends.

Certainly, puppy play-biting behavior must be eliminated eventually. We cannot have an adult dog playfully mauling family, friends, and strangers in the manner of a young pup. However, puppy play-biting behavior must be eliminated gradually and progressively, via a systematic process.

Most important, your puppy must be taught to control the force of its bites before play-biting behavior is eliminated altogether.

Mitty patiently teaches "Off" to Phoenie and Oso. Calm, playful cats are very adept at teaching puppies to play gently, to tone down the force of their bites, and to develop a soft mouth.

1. Inhibiting the Force of Bites

The first item on the agenda is to stop your puppy from hurting people. It is not necessary to punish the pup, but it is essential to let your pup know when its bites hurt. A simple "Ouch!" and a short time-out from play are usually sufficient. The severity of the "Ouch!" should vary according to the severity of the pain and your puppy's mental make-up.

If your puppy acknowledges its over-zealous munch, instruct it to come, sit, and stay, and then resume playing.

If, however, your puppy ignores your yelp and simply bites again, turn away, and verbally express your displeasure, "Ouch!!! That hurt! You miserable worm." For added effect, you may accentuate your injured feelings by sobbing. Whatever you do to get the point across that you are hurt and upset, never shout at, or physically punish your pup. Invariably, this would make matters worse. With many breeds, shouting, screaming, and physical punishment only serve to make a puppy more excited, causing it to bite more vigorously. Also, physical punishment will likely cause your puppy to become fearful and aggressive, leading to a far more serious kind of biting. Puppy abuse creates aggression.

If you feel your puppy still ignores your feedback, call it a "Jerk!", leave the room, and shut the door. Make sure you play with your puppy in its long-term confinement area, so that it cannot get up to

Playful adult dogs are very adept at teaching puppies to play roughly, but to bite gently.

any mischief when left alone. (See Chapter 6, "Household Etiquette." If your puppy does not heed your feedback, you are out of control. Consequently, it would not be wise to take your puppy by the collar to lead it to its long-term confinement area.) Leave the long-term confinement area without touching your puppy and give it some time to calm down. Allow your puppy just a one- or two-minute time-out to reflect on the loss of its favorite human playmate, then return to make up before resuming play. You want to demonstrate that you still love your puppy and that it is only the painful bites that you find objectionable. Call your puppy and have it sit while you talk to it calmly and hand-feed several pieces of kibble to practice "Off" and "Gently."

If you feel your puppy's biting behavior is getting out of hand, schedule a home consultation with a Certified Pet Dog Trainer (CPDT) and enroll in a puppy training class. To find a CPDT in your area, contact the Association of Pet Dog Trainers at www.apdt.com or 1-800-PET-DOGS.

Once your puppy's "bites" no longer hurt, it is time to tone down jaw pressure entirely. While your puppy is munching away on your hands, wait for a nibble that is harder than the rest and then respond as if it really hurt (even though it didn't) "Ouch! Gennntly! That hurt me, you bully!" Your puppy will begin to think "Good Heavens! These humans are really namby pamby – I can bite baby puppies harder than that! These humans are soooooo sensitive, I'll have to be

Nonetheless, uneducated puppies can still be a bit of a pain.

really careful when mouthing their delicate skin." And that's precisely what you want your puppy to think. You want your pup to be extremely careful when playing with people. Ideally, your pup should have learned not to hurt people before it is four months old, and it should no longer be exerting any mouthing pressure whatsoever well before it is five months old.

2. Inhibiting the Incidence of Mouthing

Once your puppy has learned to mouth gently rather than biting during play, start reducing the frequency of your pup's mouthing behavior. Teach your pup that mouthing is OK until you request it to stop. Why? Because it is inconvenient to try to drink a cup of tea or answer the telephone with fifty pounds of pup dangling from your wrist. That's why. This is yet another useful application for "Off."

Teach "Off" as described in the hand-feeding exercises. Once your puppy understands the meaning of the instruction, "Off" may be used effectively to stop mouthing. When playing with your puppy, say "Off!" Praise your pup when it lets go and offer a piece of kibble.

The essence of this exercise is to practice stopping your puppy from mouthing; each time your puppy stops mouthing, resume playing and then you can practice stopping again. Also, because your puppy really enjoys play-mouthing, the best reward for stopping is allowing it to start again, i.e., let your pup resume mouthing as a reward for obediently having stopped mouthing on request. Stop and start the play session many times over and you will quickly establish control over your puppy's rambunctious behavior.

When you decide to stop the mouthing session altogether, simply say "Let's get a cookie." Heel your pup to the kitchen and give it a freeze-dried liver treat and then a stuffed Kong to occupy its jaws.

By the time your pup is five months old, it should not be exerting any pressure when mouthing, and it should stop mouthing immediately upon request by any family member.

Unsolicited mouthing is essential for puppies, but barely acceptable for a young adolescent dog, and utterly inappropriate for an older adolescent or adult dog. No matter how playful its intentions, it would be absolutely unacceptable for a six-month-old dog to take hold of a child's arm to solicit attention. This sort of situation gives parents the heebie-jeebies and gets even friendly dogs into very deep trouble.

Now you must teach your puppy never to mouth any person unless requested. Neither should your puppy be allowed to mouth hair, shoelaces, ties, trousers, skirts, or any other article of clothing. Hair and clothing have no feelings, and therefore do not elicit the necessary, appropriate feedback to let the puppy know that it is biting too hard and too close to human skin.

Children

For puppy-owners with children, the next few months present a bit of a challenge—an infinitely worthwhile challenge, because puppies growing up with children generally develop exceedingly sound temperaments. They have to! When pups grow up in constant contact with children, there is little in life to surprise or upset them later on. However, to optimize the relationship between your puppy and children, and to make sure your pup develops a good nature and solid disposition, you must educate your children as well as your puppy.

For puppy owners without a ready supply of children, socialization presents a more challenging problem. You need to recruit some little human playmates and invite them over to play with your puppy. Waste no time. Teaching puppies to love children is urgent and important.

Teaching Children
How to Act Around Puppies

Children seem to do just about everything possible to excite dogs and incite them to give chase and play roughly. Children make rapid, uncoordinated movements—running, jumping, skipping, dashing to and fro, and falling over. Children have flailing arms and hands which grab, tug, hug, squeeze, pat, prod, and thump. Children generate lots of noise with shouts, high-pitched squeaks, and shrill screams. Rather than telling children not to do this and not to do that, it is better to use positive counterconditioning. For example, ask children to sit or stand still, speak softly, keep their hands by their sides, and move slowly whenever around puppies and dogs.

Enforce a simple rule for all people (adults included): If someone wants to play with the pup, he/she must first ask the puppy if it wants to play. How? By requesting the puppy to come and sit. If the puppy neither comes nor sits when requested, further interaction with this individual would be unwise. Apparently the puppy doesn't want to know the person, and obviously the person cannot control the pup. With continued interaction, the puppy would only learn bad habits for which, no doubt, it will be punished later in life. The person (child or adult) needs a quickie education regarding how to control puppies before being allowed to play with your puppy.

Children need to be taught how to control your puppy using training techniques that are suitable for children. Off-leash lure/reward techniques are the answer since they do not involve touching the dog, and therefore physical strength and coordination are unnecessary. Even though a child may be laughing and giggling as your puppy approaches and sits with a waggy tail, the child is indeed controlling the pup, and your pup is showing compliance and beginning to respect children. Lure/reward techniques allow children to succeed. And success does wonders for children's self-esteem.

Moreover, the wonderful side-effect of lure/reward training is that your puppy learns to like children, because during training it receives plenty of food rewards. In fact, when teaching dogs to like children, the use of food lures and rewards should be mandatory.

Teaching Puppies How to Act around Children

Teaching children how to train and control your puppy teaches your puppy to like children, and how to act in a controlled manner around children. Meeting children in this fashion helps your puppy build confidence.

Each day invite a different child to come by to feed your puppy its dinner. Teach your puppy to sit automatically when greeting children. Sitting to greet children is socially acceptable. Jumping up is not. Mix some of your pup's dried kibble with some freeze-dried liver treats in a plastic bag and give it to the child. Demonstrate how to use a food lure to entice the pup to sit and how the puppy will not take food until instructed to "Take It." Then, standing behind the child with your hand around theirs, have the child call the puppy and offer a treat from the palm of their hand.

With appropriate guidance, even extremely young children can enjoy success with lure/reward training techniques.

Jamie likes Phoenix. Phoenix likes Jamie. But Phoenix did not find it amusing when Jamie and Isaac went hunting Malamute with water cannons. However, Phoenix readily forgave them both after five freeze-dried liver treats.

Have the child repeatedly back up and instruct the pup to come and sit, making sure that the puppy does sit each time before being offered the food. Once your pup eagerly comes and sits whenever requested, put it on leash and have the child repeatedly back away and approach the puppy to give it a treat when it sits. In no time at all, your puppy will learn to sit automatically whenever it sees a child approaching. In fact, your puppy may sit to entice children to approach.

Then have the child hold your pup's bowl of kibble and periodically offer ultra-scrumptious treats. This way your puppy learns that regardless of the contents of its bowl, children usually have something better to offer. From your puppy's point of view, this is the training exercise to beat all exercises. In fact, this type of training "exercise" is so rewarding, and so much fun for everyone, you should arrange a training party for your puppy.

No matter how well-trained and good-natured your puppy and no matter how well-trained your children, never leave them together unsupervised. Especially be careful when your well trained, good-natured child's friends come to visit. Two children have the activity of three, and three children can reach critical mass—emitting energy levels unmeasurable by any scientific instrument.

Puppy Parties

To make sure your puppy meets lots of people in a controlled and non-threatening setting, host a Puppy Party at home. In addition to being one of most important items on your puppy's educational agenda, socializing your puppy is certainly the most enjoyable endeavor.

Puppy time is party time and sharing time. Do not be a big blue meanie and keep your puppy all to yourself. Introduce it to family, friends, and neighbors, and especially to children and men. Invite them over in packs for a series of Puppy Parties. Entice the children with balloons, streamers, party hats, presents, candy, and cake. Entice the men with beer, football games on the TV, or compliments. (Men are extremely easy to train, I have been informed.) Do whatever it takes...but get this puppy socialized!

After being removed from Mum and its littermates at about six to eight weeks of age, your puppy has to be kept isolated from the outside world until it has had its inoculations (against Distemper, Parvovirus, and other serious diseases). Your puppy must be at least three months old before it can safely venture outdoors onto public property, and so there is a necessary, but nonetheless gaping hiatus in your puppy's socialization with other dogs. Your puppy can make up for its lost doggy playtime during puppy training classes. However, do not neglect your puppy's socialization with humans.

Invite people by to meet your puppy. Still maintain routine hygiene, though. Instruct all guests to leave outdoor shoes outside and wash their hands before playing with your pup.

Teach the children how to act around your puppy and teach the pup how to act around children. Remember, it is usually neighborhood children who terrorize dogs through the garden fence—exciting and inciting the dogs to bark, growl, snap, and lunge. And then it is the same children's parents—your neighbors—who complain because your dog is barking. Children are less likely to terrorize a dog they know and like, as they are less likely to terrorize a dog owned by people they know and like. Consequently, do your very best to get to know your neighborhood children by inviting them to get to know your puppy.

It's socialization time for the cat and dogs and Halloween children

It's party-time! But still think of your puppy's waistline. Weigh out your pup's daily food allowance (kibble plus freeze-dried liver treats). Sprinkle some freeze-dried liver powder over the kibble and then you have the ideal training treat—irresistible to your puppy's nose, yet highly nutritious. ("Junk-food" treats would cause your puppy to develop a liver like a goose.) Divide the food into little plastic bags and give one to each party guest to hand-feed to your pup so that your pup learns that strangers are a lot of fun and that human hands are good news. Make sure to include a greater proportion of freeze-dried liver treats in each of the children's and men's baggies, so that your puppy learns especially to enjoy the presence and presents of children and men.

Once your puppy happily accepts food treats from party guests, and has an indelibly wonderful first impression of children and men, it is time for you to train your guests to train your puppy for you. (See the previous chapter on Good Manners.)

From now on, your pup has to come and sit before receiving any more food rewards so that it learns to sit automatically when approached. As early as possible, establish sitting as the status quo for greeting people. Sitting beats jumping up. And from your dog's point of view, sitting for prospective treats certainly beats being punished for jumping up!

Pass the Puppy

While we have all these people conveniently at hand, it's time to play Pass the Puppy. Each person will have the opportunity to handle, gentle, and examine the puppy in turn. Each person should introduce themself to the puppy using the Casablanca technique—"Hello! I'm a stranger and here's a treat"—before proceeding to examine the pup in a similar rewarding fashion. "Let's look in your ear—here's another treat. Let's look in the other ear—here's one more. Open your mouth. My! What big teeth you have. A big treat for those. Let's feel these paws—one treat for each. And let's examine those private parts—two treats for those." Then pass the puppy to the left. After being handled by several people in turn, the puppy is in good stead to be examined by a veterinarian, or even to be hugged and handled by children.

The first couple of parties should be fairly sedate affairs to give your young pup the opportunity to get used to the invasion of people. Thereafter, however, it is important to make each Puppy Party a festive occasion. Balloons, streamers, party-favors, noise-makers, and fun and games are de rigeur.

It is so important your puppy be thoroughly accustomed to children running around and screaming, because that's what children

What is the point of living with a dog that you cannot cuddle? Living with dogs we daren't touch is about as silly as living with people we daren't touch. Make sure that your puppy develops the confidence to thoroughly enjoy being handled by family, friends, and strangers, and especially by children, veterinarians, and groomers. Women don't bite gynecologists, and shy men don't punch hair stylists. We don't attack our health and beauty care personnel and neither would dogs, if only they were adequately socialized as puppies. It must be so terrifying for a dog to be scared of people, and to be

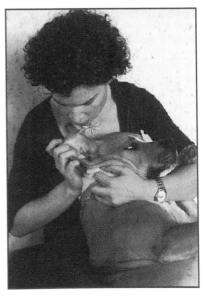

do. If the dog is already an adolescent before it sees its first child running and screaming in the park, generally we are in for trouble. Either the dog will run and chase it its eagerness to join in, or the dog will run and hide out of fear. Neither is a healthy prospect. However, for the lucky puppy who has attended numerous Puppy Parties and seen children (or adults) laughing, screaming, running, skipping, and falling over...well, that's just old hat—like totally boring, dude! Been there, done that! After several Puppy Parties it is highly unlikely that anything in real life will be as weird as what has become the snoring-boring established status quo of Puppy Parties.

As soon as your puppy is old enough to safely go to public places, it's high time to enroll in a puppy training class.

Also, take regular long walks around the neighborhood and visit the local dog parks. Give your puppy ample opportunity to develop the confidence to enjoy being a dog.

CHAPTER SIX
Household Etiquette

Before your young pup can be trusted to have full run of your house and garden, somebody has to teach it household rules. And that somebody is you! If you don't, no doubt your puppydog will happily let imagination wander wild in its quest for suitable occupational therapy to pass the time of day. Without a firm grounding in canine domestic etiquette, your puppy will be forced to improvise in its choice of toys and its choice of toilets. Your puppy will probably pee and poop on carpets, and curtains will be viewed as mere playthings.

If your young pup is allowed to make *any* mistakes, "bad" habits will quickly become the norm. And then, you will have to break bad habits before instilling new ones.

Attention and management are the hallmarks of a successful domestic education. When you are physically (or mentally) absent, confine your puppy to keep it out of mischief. When you are not at home, keep it confined to a fairly small area with a comfortable bed, a supply of fresh water, plenty of chewtoys, and a doggy toilet. Obviously, your pup may feel the need to relieve itself, chew, or bark during the course of the day, so it is best left in a place where these activities will not cause annoyance to yourself, your family, or your

When away from home, confine your puppy to a playroom with a comfy bed, a bowl of water, some chewtoys stuffed with kibble, and a doggy toilet. Long-term confinement prevents mistakes around the house, encourages your puppy to use its toilet, and teaches your puppy to settle down and chew

neighbors. One purpose of long-term confinement is to confine the pup's behavior to a protected area so that its natural habits do not become a problem. Another purpose of long-term confinement is to maximize the likelihood that your puppy will develop a chewtoy habit (the only chewables in its confinement area), and so learn to settle down and pass the time quietly and calmly.

It is better to leave your puppy indoors—in the kitchen, a bathroom, or a utility room. Do not to let your unattended puppy have full run of the yard, or it will most certainly become an indiscriminate barker, chewer, and digger, and will soil anywhere it pleases. This type of pup is much more difficult to housetrain later on, and in all probability, will never be allowed indoors as an adult. If it is necessary to leave your puppy outdoors, leave it in a specially constructed dog run, with numerous chewtoys for amusement.

When you are present, pay attention to your pup. Good habits must become routine. Each mistake is a potential disaster since it sets the precedent for many more to come. So watch your puppy at all times! It is unwise to take your eyes off a young puppy for more than a second. It is far easier to watch your puppy if it is settled down in one spot, for example in its dog bed. I used to tell Phoenix to settle down right in front of the television, or beside me when I wrote on the computer. Thus, it is possible to ration only a single neuron to keep an eye on the dog. (In fact, I like to think she's here now. "Hey, Phoenie! Daddy's still writing about you!") If it proves to be too much brain-strain to keep an eye on your puppy, put it on leash. Either tie the leash to your belt and have the dog settle down at your feet, or fasten the leash to an eye-hook in the baseboard.

If you are too busy, or too preoccupied to pay full attention to your puppy, confine it. Leave your puppy in its long-term confinement area to help it become accustomed to being left alone when you are away. (See Home Alone section). Or, put your puppy into a short-term, close-confinement area (such as a dog crate) with several chewtoys. A dog crate may be moved from room to room. The intention is not to lock up your puppy for hours on end, but rather to teach it to settle down quickly in a variety of settings and to remain there for variable-length but relatively short periods.

Short-term close confinement prevents many behavioral problems for a limited period of time. For example, while lying in its den, a dog cannot dig in the garden, soil the bedroom, or destroy the house, and it will be less likely to bark. Additionally, short-term close confinement techniques are a boon for training dogs to like chewtoys, and for predicting when your puppy wants to eliminate (the key to successful housetraining).

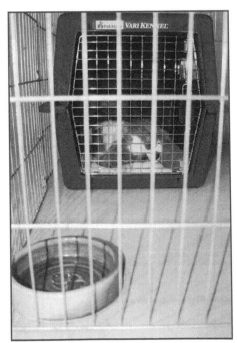

When you are at home, unless you can devote one hundred percent attention to your puppy, confine the pup to a doggy den with some chewtoys stuffed with kibble. Short-term confinement prevents mistakes around the house, teaches your puppy to chew chewtoys calmly and quietly (so that it does not become anxious, or develop a barking habit), and allows you to accurately predict when your pup needs to relieve itself. Every hour on the hour, lead your puppy to an appropriate toilet area and it will eliminate within three minutes. Praise your pup

Housetraining

Right from the outset, do not let your puppy make any mistakes. There are three reasons for this. First, only one pee or poop doth a habit make. Second, not only is the little doggie relieving itself, it is also scent marking, and despite the claims of many commercial odor eliminators, dog urine leaves an indelible scent that forever screams out to a multitude of eager neurons leading from nose to brain to bladder, "Pee here again!" Third, even a single deposit is a mess to clean up.

Housesoiling is a matter of bad placement. Location! Location! Location! Housesoiling is just an example of a normal, natural, and necessary doggy behavior occurring in the "wrong" (inappropriate) place. Thus housetraining is quickly and easily accomplished by praising your puppy and offering a food reward for going in the right place. Once your pup realizes its by-products are the equivalent of coins in a food vending machine—tokens which the pup may cash in for food rewards simply by relieving itself in a designated area—your puppy will not want to eliminate anywhere else. Instead, your dog will want to choose the appropriate spot, since to go anywhere else, or to soil the house when you are away, would be a woeful waste of urine and feces that does not produce equivalent fringe benefits.

By offering graduated rewards, you may train your puppy to use a highly specific doggy toilet area. Vary the level of the reward according to how close your pup approximates "ground zero." Start with a "Good dog!" each time it does it outside. Then a "Good dog!!" and an ear scratch for doing it within twenty feet of the target. A "Gooood dog!!!", several pats, and a piece of kibble if it manages to get within ten feet. And for scoring a bull's-eye, three liver treats, a "Goooood little doggie!!!!", multiple scratches and pats, a barbecued sheep for supper, extra TV privileges, and a free trip to the Bahamas! One can never afford to be a master of understatement when housetraining a dog or a child.

Housesoiling is also a matter of bad timing. Either your puppy is in the wrong place at the right time (indoors with full bladder and bowels), or it is in the right place at the wrong time (outdoors with empty bladder and bowels).

When you are not at home, confine your puppy in an area with a doggy toilet. When you are at home, confine your puppy to a crate so that you may accurately predict when it

Timing is the *sine qua non* of successful housetraining. Indeed, efficient and effective housetraining depends upon you being able to predict *when* your puppy needs to go. Only then may you direct your puppy to the appropriate spot and reward it for doing the right thing in the right place at the right time.

Short-term close confinement offers a convenient means of accurately making this prediction. When a puppy is confined to a small area, it is temporarily (for about 90 minutes) inhibited from urinating or defecating. Understandably, the pup does not want to soil its sleeping area. Hence, the puppy is highly likely to want to go immediately after being released from confinement.

When at home, keep your puppy on leash indoors, or confined to its bed or crate. Every hour release the pup and say "Outside!" Then quickly run your pup to the chosen toilet area—on leash if necessary. But hurry! *Vitement! Schnell! Pronto!* No room for plantigrade plodders here—otherwise your puppy may pee or poop *en route*. Instruct your pup to relieve itself, by saying "Hurry up!", "Do your business," or whatever socially-acceptable, euphemistic eliminatory command you have chosen. I generally say, "Pee and poop for a cookie!" Give your puppydog three minutes to oblige. Usually a young pup will urinate within less than a minute, and often defecate within one or two minutes. (Bladder and bowels have filled up during confinement and running your pup to the doggy toilet has jiggled everything around.) Once success is in your hands (and puppy pee or poop is in the toilet area), praise your puppy extravagantly. Tell your pup what a most wonderful and glorious thing it has done. Offer a couple of food rewards, play with your puppy, or take it for a walk as a well-deserved reward.

What if your puppy fails to perform within the allotted time span. Hey! No big deal! Just take the pup back indoors to its close confinement area for another hour. Then repeat the process every hour. Eventually, your puppy will achieve success and be handsomely rewarded for its trouble. "Hey! No trouble!" says the pup. Thus, your puppy's appropriate behavior is progressively reinforced and it learns what is expected when it hears the instructions "Outside!" and "Hurry Up!" Your puppy has learned to go on command.

Regardless of whether your puppy has been trained to eliminate in the backyard, or at curbside, a walk is one of the best rewards for a defecating dog. People with fenced yards seldom use this valuable reward at all. Neither for that matter do most people who customarily take their dogs outside to eliminate on public property. The common practice of walking a dog to induce it to relieve itself is quite awry. The dog gets the walk for free and often the walk is terminated as soon as the dog has performed its task. So the dog gets one of the biggest rewards in the civilized canine world (a walk) for doing no more than acting like the proverbial banana in expectation of going walkies, yet it receives the biggest punishment in domestic dogdom (termination of said walk) for doing the right thing in the right place at the right time! We seem to be 180 degrees out of phase here.

Instead, release your dog from confinement, take it outside and wait for three minutes. If your dog does not do what is required, put it back in its close confinement area for another hour. However, if your dog does eliminate, it is much more convenient to clean up your dog's mess and dispose of it in your own trash can before setting off for a walk than it is to is stroll around the neighborhood clutching a bag of doggie doo. Additionally, your dog may receive the walk as a reward for defecating. You will find that a no feces–no walk philosophy creates a very speedy defecator. Now your puppy will want to relieve itself when and where you want.

The potential number of mistakes has been decimated. However, should you ever catch your puppy in the act of soiling the house, a verbal rebuke is sufficient—"Spot, Outside! Outside!" Or for the literary-minded, "Out, damned Spot!" Always be instructive when reprimanding your dog. Try to convey the necessary two pieces of information in a single word, e.g., "Outside!" The urgent tone informs Spot he is about to make a mistake, and the meaning of the word instructs Spot as to the appropriate location for toilet activity. Remember, it is not the act of urinating or defecating that is wrong, but rather it's just that we humans consider an inside location to be inappropriate.

Physical punishments are quite uncalled for. In fact, take care not to go overboard with the reprimand itself. The goal is to turn the mistake into a learning experience by emphasizing the appropriate location, not to scramble your poor pup's brains. If you frighten your dog it may feel reluctant to go in your presence again, and this will make housetraining very tricky indeed. Indeed, your puppy will feel compelled to relieve itself only in your absence: for example, in the living room after you have left for work, or even worse, in your bedroom after you've taken the dog for a walk!

If you come home to find a mess on the floor, just clean up the mess and forget about scolding your dog. It's too late for your dog to make the connection between an idiopathic owner temper tantrum and its having relieved itself sometime earlier. If you punished the dog after the act, it would simply learn that it was silly to greet you and come within arm's reach. Next time, perhaps it won't. If you want to punish someone, punish yourself, "Bad owner! Bad owner!" You

Instruct your puppy to pee and poop before going for a walk. Elimination close to home facilitates clean-up and disposal. And now, the start of the walk may be used as a reward for eliminating on request. A "no feces–no walk" policy quickly produces a very speedy defecator.

should never have allowed an unhousetrained dog to have the run of the house. What on earth were you thinking?

Obviously, never do anything as cruel, or as stupid, as rubbing your puppy's nose in the feces—that is, unless your training goal is to teach your dog to mash feces into the carpet, or to use its nose to shovel the feces from room to room.

Chewing

Chewing mistakes can be extremely expensive. A single chewing spree can cause damage that easily runs into thousands of dollars. My most expensive case history involved an Akita, which inflicted $10,000 worth of damage to the interior of a Mercedes in less than half an hour. Chewing is no problem for the dog, but, depending on what it's chewing, it can be a big problem for the owner. Consequently, have a good supply of chewtoys on hand, and teach your puppy what they are for. In fact, have a toy box permanently accessible so your puppy always knows where it can find a toy should it be in need of a quick chew. Above all praise your puppy each and every time it plays with one of its toys.

An easy way to get your puppy hooked on chewtoys is to make a habit of having the pup settle down in its dog bed or crate with plenty of chewtoys within reach. In fact, the thinking owner would make

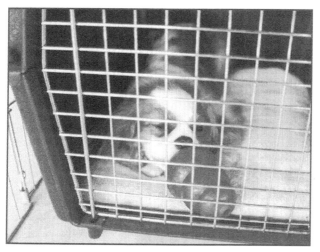

Unless your puppy can be trusted to have full run of the house, keep the pup confined as much as possible with chewtoys stuffed with kibble. Your puppy will teach itself to chew chewtoys and soon develop a chewtoy

Chewtoys should be indestructible. Squeaky toys are not chewtoys! Squeaky toys are marvellous for teaching bite inhibition. When playing with your pup, pretend that the squeaky is a live animal and teach your pup not to hurt it.

sure the only objects within reach are chewtoys. Thus your puppy develops a serious chewtoy habit right from the outset, if only because there is precious little else to chew.

Chewtoys should be indestructible. If chewtoys are easily destroyed, they will need to be replaced. This costs money. Also, it is not good for your puppy to consume non-food items. Kong products and sterilized long bones (both commercially available in pet stores) are good resilient chewtoys for most dogs. As both of these are hollow, they may be stuffed with goodies to heighten your pup's interest and entice it to chew. Stuff chewtoys with three types of goodies: kibble which comes out easily, kibble which takes some time for your dog to extricate, and freeze-dried liver which the dog can never get out.

Thus your puppy is rewarded the instant it investigates a chewtoy and again and again as it works on it for a while. It will then continue to busy itself with the chewtoy knowing the tastiest treats are still stuck inside. For example, different shaped biscuits are ideal for stuffing Kongs and Biscuit Balls. Some shaped biscuits go in and come out easily, whereas other shaped biscuits have to be forced in and require human fingers to pull them out.

Prepare a number of stuffed chewtoys for your puppy for whenever you ask it to settle down, or whenever you leave it on its own. Your puppy will happily worry at the chewtoys until it falls asleep. When you return, delay greeting your puppy until it fetches a chewtoy. Then pull out the treats remaining in the Kong and give them to your pup. You will find that when your dog wakes up in the afternoon and becomes active in anticipation of your return, it will go in search of a chewtoy. To this day, Oso will always search for a big red Kong before greeting me at the front door.

Once your puppydog has developed a strong chewtoy habit, it is worthwhile to pause to consider a few of the things a dog cannot be doing while busying itself with a chewtoy.

Once your puppy learns what it should be chewing, chewing catastrophes will be minimal. On occasion, though, it may be necessary to let your dog know what it should not be chewing. Every time your pup even sniffs a likely target, the instructive reprimand "Chewtoy!" should quickly set it straight. The tone (soft but firm) informs the pup that it is about to make a mistake, and the word instructs your pup what it should be chewing.

"My name is Claude and I'm a Kongaholic! Kongs saved my life. I used to eat basketballs, which had to be surgically removed. Messy! Dangerous! After I was adopted from the SF SPCA, all my food—breakfast and dinner—was served stuffed inside Kongs and bones. Dining from Kongs allowed me to take the time to savor dinner, which was good because I was not allowed to gorge—nasty stomach scarring from the basketballs. I still like the occasional meal in a Kong. Eating from Kongs is a bit of a challenge. But I

David Letterdog's List of Things
Dogs Cannot Do While Chewing a Chewtoy

1   Chew carpets, curtains, cushions, couches, clothes, chair legs, children's toys, electrical cords, and computer disks. Play-bite (or mouth) human hands, arms, legs, and ankles. Play tug o' war with trousers, skirts, and shoe laces.

2   Surf kitchen counters. Empty cupboards. Lick butter from the refrigerator. Trash the trash.

3   Dig in the yard for escape or enjoyment. (Certainly a dog can dig while holding a chewtoy in its jaws, but if really working on its chewtoy it will have little time for digging holes. And it will not want to bury its chewtoy with the tastiest treats still inside.)

4   Destroy the yard, chew garden furniture and fences, eat flowers and poisonous plants, truffle for cat feces.

5   Become overly anxious or bored when home alone. Escape from solitary isolation in the yard (through the dismantled fence). Obsessively and compulsively stare at a blank wall, or chase its tail and run in ever-decreasing circles.

6   Bark for the sake of barking. (The dog may still alarm bark at disturbances. But it will be less likely to bark recreationally if it is busy chewing recreationally.)

7   Grab the leash and jerk back.

8   Drive the car, cross dress, and run up credit card balances. (Just checking to see if anyone is actually reading this list.)

9   Gnaw its paws and chew the root of its tail, aggravating flea allergies and inflaming "hot spots." Or otherwise indulge in noisy personal hygiene in the company of visitors.

10 Annoy other animals. Bait, bother, badger, or bully other dogs. Pester, plague, provoke, tease, trouble or torture cats and children. And otherwise be a pain.

Digging

Dogs need to dig. There are a dozen *bona fide* canine reasons for digging, including burying bones and digging them up again. However, from the people point of view, dogs invariably dig in the wrong place. Consequently, to be fair, provide a digging pit (much like a child's sandbox), and then teach your dog to use it.

Keep the digging pit stocked with enticements: food treats, stashes of kibble, Kongs, marrow bones, and other stuffed chewtoys (yes, we need them outdoors, too). Once your dog learns that its digging pit is a virtual treasure trove, it will prefer to dig there than anywhere else in the yard. After all, what's so marvelous about unearthing a root, or a worm, when there are all sorts of goodies to be found in the pit? For example, just imagine your dog's amazement on finding a meaty cow's femur buried in its digging pit. I mean, in 1849 thousands of people flocked to California because one person found a piece of gold at Sutter's Mill. They didn't rush to New Jersey, did they? The gold was discovered in California. Similarly, your dog is likely to dig most holes in its digging pit, where a cow's femur was once discovered.

If you ever intend to leave your puppy unattended in your yard or garden, you must teach it garden rules. Spend some time in the yard with your puppy. For example, your pup must be taught never even to walk on the flower beds, let alone dig in them. It may walk and lie down on the lawn, but if you should see your dog about to dig there, the instructive reprimand "Digging Pit!" informs your dog both that it is doing something wrong and where it should dig to make it right.

Barking

Surely, no one would think of putting a shock-collar on a canary for tweeting, squirting lemon juice into a baby's mouth for crying, or beating a husband with a rolled up newspaper for "singing" in the shower. However, people think nothing of doing all of these things and more to barking dogs. If they didn't want barking, perhaps they should have considered a plant as a pet! Of course dogs bark. Barking is a perfectly normal and respectable doggy behavior. In fact, barking is the quintessence of the canine repertoire. It would be unfair (and utterly asinine) to try to stop dogs from barking altogether. Instead, owners should prevent barking from becoming a temporal problem. Prevent your dog from barking excessively and from barking at inappropriate times.

Barking poses particular problems because owners are consistently inconsistent. Sometimes the dog is allowed to bark. Sometimes it is encouraged to bark. Yet other times it is severely punished for barking. It is all so confusing and stressful for the poor dog. No wonder it lets rip when the owner is away from the house. It is easier and less confusing for both the owner and dog to start with a single rule, "Barking is OK, until requested to shush!" After being asked to "Shush!" the dog is expected to be quiet for a specified time—say one or two minutes. (By then, most dogs have forgotten why they were barking in the first place.)

The first step in teaching your puppy to reduce barking is to teach it to bark on command. This may sound silly, but obviously it would be impossible to practice stopping your dog from barking if it were not already barking. Now we all know it is an extremely difficult prospect to quiet a dog when it excitedly barks at inconvenient times. For example, when your dog is all worked up barking at some nocturnal critter at three in the morning. The dog really wants to continue barking, and the middle of the night is not the best of times for patient tuition from most owners. Instead, by training your dog to speak on cue, you may practice teaching it to shush at times which are most convenient for you. By so doing, "shush training" becomes a less daunting prospect because most probably your dog never wanted to bark in the first place. Barking was your idea!

Once you can turn your dog "on and off" at will, it becomes possible to modify your dog's barking sprees by teaching it when you would like it to bark, how long you would like it to bark, and when you would like it to be quiet.

Training Your Dog to Woof on Cue

1   Select a stimulus that prompts your puppy to bark, e.g., the door bell. Station an accomplice outside the front door and then instruct your puppy to "Woof!" or "Speak!"

2   This is the cue for your accomplice to ring the door bell.

3   Your puppy will bark as soon as it hears the doorbell.

After several repetitions, your puppy learns that your command "Woof!" always predicts that the doorbell is about to ring. Consequently, your pup will begin to bark at your request in anticipation of the doorbell. Well done! You have taught your puppy to bark on command.

This type of exercise might give a guard dog an insecurity complex. "How on earth does my owner know when the doorbell is going to ring? They get it right every time. I'm going to bark when the owner says 'Woof!' just to ensure job security."

Woof-Shush Sequences

1   Ask your puppy to bark and praise it profusely for doing so. This practice alone comes as a pleasant surprise to many dogs. Join in with the chorus if you like.

2   After a few woofs, instruct your puppy to "Shush."

3   Waggle a food lure in front of its nose.

4   As soon as your puppy sniffs the food, it will stop barking. Praise it gently for sniffing quietly.

Food is the very best shush-lure, since it is impossible for the pup to sniff and bark at the same time. Offer a piece of kibble as a reward. Continue praising your pup as it eats—"Goooood shushhhh." Talking

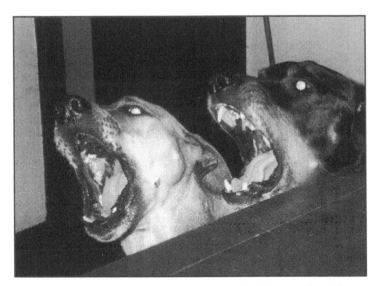

in whispers will encourage your pup to listen. If it listens, it will not bark, otherwise it will not be able to hear what it is listening to. Using a food lure to entice your puppy to sit or lie down will also help it settle calmly and quietly.

After a few seconds of glorious silence, instruct your pup to bark again—a second pleasant surprise for the dog. Now tell it to shush once more. No matter how difficult it was to get your dog to be quiet the first time, it will be much easier the second. Then tell it to bark again—"Good boy, Joe Pup, good woofs. Wrroo, wrroo wrrooooo!" Then instruct it to shush once more—"Gooooood boy. Goood shhhhush." That's all there is to it.

Now your Woof–Shush–trained puppy may be allowed to be a real dog, and bark until you tell it to stop. Also, you may teach your puppy other specific barking rules. Your pup may be taught to which stimuli you want it to bark (e.g., the doorbell) and to which stimuli it is permitted to bark (e.g., a cat in the yard—come on, let's be fair! And anyway, surely you don't want your neighbor's cat to requisition your garden as an outdoor litter box). You may teach your pup how long it is allowed to bark in each instance (five or six woofs are usually quite enough). And, you may teach your pup when it is not allowed to bark (e.g., when a leaf falls three blocks away—hardly a world-shattering event that needs to be heralded by several hundred woofs).

Home Alone

It is natural for people to want their pup to be perfectly well behaved and to amuse itself when left at home alone. However, some owners expect the pup to act like a perfect angel with nary a hint of what's required. It's almost as if owners know how they want the puppy to behave but intentionally keep it a secret, only to moan and groan when the little rascal predictably finds doggy ways to amuse itself. They expect the puppy to learn household manners on its own. We call this the Lassie Syndrome, whereby owners harbor the misassumption that puppies come fully trained with Lassie-like abilities—to go for help, to fix household appliances, and to be perfectly behaved when left at home alone for hours on end. Sorry to burst your bubble, but this is television fiction. Somebody has to train your puppy how to appropriately amuse itself when left at home alone, and that somebody is you!

For most owners there are times when it is necessary to leave the puppydog at home alone. If you expect your puppy to be well behaved and to settle down when you are gone, there are two things you must do. First, make sure your puppy is well behaved and knows how to settle down at times when you are present. Obviously, you can only train your puppy when you there. Consequently, when you are home, teach your pup how you expect it to act when you are gone. Second, prepare your puppy to enjoy spending some quiet time alone before confining it for long periods.

Dogs are crepuscular. They have two activity peaks during the day—at dawn and at dusk. Most dogs are quite happy to sleep through the night and to settle down and snooze away the middle of the day. However, some dogs are not. Some dogs require some form of occupational therapy to pass the time of day. If appropriate entertainment (stuffed chewtoys) is not provided, the dog will be forced to improvise, and will no doubt resort to doggy activities (urine marking, chewing, digging, barking) to pass the time of day.

Separation Anxiety

Some dogs become anxious and stressed when left at home alone. Canine anxiety is bad news—for owners, and for dogs. When dogs are stressed, otherwise normal behaviors become repctitive, stereotypical, and compulsive. Urination, defecation, pacing/running to and fro, chewing, digging, and barking may all increase in frequency to the extent that normal doggy behaviors become annoying behavior problems. Equally worrying, being anxious is not much fun for the dog.

Ironically, much of the dog's stress and anxiety has been unintentionally created by well-meaning owners. Constantly smothering your pup with affection when you are at home makes it far more likely to miss your attentions when you are gone. If your puppy becomes over-dependent on your presence, it may become over-anxious at times when you are away. Make sure that you take the time to build your puppy's confidence so that it enjoys the time that it spends by itself.

To prepare your puppy for confinement in your absence, make sure to regularly confine your puppy when you are home. With regular short-term, close confinement, your puppy will quickly learn household manners, and it will develop the confidence to stand on its own four paws when you are not around. Also, when you are home, occasionally confine your puppy to its long-term confinement area, so that confinement to this area is not always associated with your absence. In addition, occasional long-term confinement when you are around allows you to monitor your pup's behavior and occasionally reward it for being good.

Make sure to provide plenty of stuffed chewtoys when leaving your puppy in its short-term and long-term confinement areas. If the

pup is gainfully preoccupied, it will fret less over your absence. Leave the radio or television playing. The sound will mask outside disturbances and provide reassurance, since radio and television are normally associated with your presence. (Phoenie was quite partial to Country Western and Golden-Oldie stations, and Oso likes National Public Radio and CNN.) Leaving a pair of used running socks (emanating concentrated wafts of *eau de owner*) outside the door of the confinement area will also reassure your puppy. Your puppy will become less anxious if it has plenty to do to keep it occupied (stuffed chewtoys), if it can smell your scent, and if it can hear noises normally associated with your presence.

Some people have problems with the notion of confinement. So do I. Inappropriate confinement is utterly inhumane. Many puppies are given far too little education and much too much freedom during their first few weeks at home. Predictably, an unsupervised puppy will develop behavior problems (housesoiling and destructive chewing), whereupon the pup is banished from the house and confined to the yard. Predictably, a yard-confined pup will develop other behavior problems (adaptive occupational therapy). The puppy becomes an indiscriminate eliminator and an indiscriminate chewer, and it starts to dig and bark. After neighbors complain of the puppy's excessive barking, the pup is further confined to the garage or basement. Basement-confined adolescent dogs become stressed and bored and predictably react to their newly imposed solitary confinement by trashing their prison cell. Eventually, many adolescent dogs are surrendered to animal shelters, where they are confined to a cage to play the lotto of life. Sadly, each year, millions of incarcerated dogs lose the lotto of life and are ultimately confined to a coffin.

I take considerable exception to the above, altogether too-frequent, sequence of events. It is simply not right to give a young puppy total freedom, then progressively steal its freedom chunk by chunk, and progressively confine the puppy more and more restrictively until eventually the poor dog is confined to a box.

A humane and intelligent alternative would comprise total, yet temporary, confinement of your new puppy so that it may learn appropriate household manners and develop sufficient independence and confidence so that it neither misbehaves nor psychologically falls apart when left at home alone. Your puppy may be progressively granted increasing freedom from week to week. Eventually, your well-behaved and confident companion gets to enjoy complete freedom of your entire house and garden for the rest of its life.

During the first few weeks, when you are at home keep your puppy confined in its short-term close confinement area (dog crate), and when you are not at home keep your puppy in its long-term confinement area (e.g., bathroom). You may increase the size of your puppy's long-term confinement area by one room for each month that goes by without any owner-absent behavior problems. For example, for the second month, increase the confinement area (downstairs bathroom) to include the kitchen. For the third month let the puppy have full run of the downstairs bathroom, kitchen, and hallway. For

Feeding your pup from Kongs is the best way to teach it to settle calmly and not develop separation anxiety. When happily preoccupied with a stuffed chewtoy, your pup does not focus on being alone, and so doesn't stress, fret, or work itself

the fourth month, allow the puppy also to have access to the family room. Of course, if your puppy makes just one housesoiling or chewing mistake when left at home alone, temporarily (for one month) confine your puppy only to the bathroom once more, and then progressively increase its freedom by one room for every problem-free month.

Certainly, in an ideal world people would spend all day long with their puppies. However, this seldom happens. Some owners leave home to go work, to go on holiday, or to spend time in the hospital. It is not always possible to take the puppy to work, on holiday, or to the hospital. The fact of the matter is that many puppies spend a lot of time at home alone. I am neither condoning this, nor making a value judgment. The length of time a puppydog spends at home alone is an individual decision that every owner makes. Instead, I am stating that if we ever plan to leave puppies and dogs at home alone, we need to prepare them beforehand. We need to teach puppies household etiquette so they know how to act when left at home alone (without engendering the displeasure of their owners). And we need to teach puppies to enjoy occasional solitary confinement so that they do not fret or panic when left at home alone.

Separation Relief

Most owner-absent, doggy "disobedience" and wanton house destruction actually has very little to do with separation anxiety. Rather, "separation relief" would be a more accurate and descriptive term. The dog chews, digs, barks, and soils the house specifically when the owner is not there. But why? Because the dog has learned it would be foolhardy to indulge in these canine activities when its owner is home. Usually, owner-absent misbehavior is a surefire advertisement that, rather than teaching the dog how to behave, the owner has tried to suppress normal, natural, and necessary doggy behavior with punishment.

Often the term "separation anxiety" is applied to a dog who is simply not housetrained. So wise up and housetrain your dog. And, if you do think your dog might really be anxious about your absence, then follow the instructions outlined above. Being anxious is not fun.

Jumping Up

No doubt you (and your family and friends) are glad to greet your dog when you return home. Well, your dog can hardly control its eagerness to greet you and your friends. And how does your dog greet people? By jumping up! You just can't win, can you? You go to all this trouble to socialize your puppy and now it goes right over the top. Now you have an adolescent dog who is too friendly.

Actually, dogs can never be too friendly. But, they do need to be taught how to greet people in a socially acceptable fashion. Generally, people become upset when nose-prodded, pawed, pushed, mouthed, molested, or hit mid-chest by an overzealous, ill-mannered, canine greeter.

Ironically, dogs receive the highest levels of punishment for being high-spirited, and they receive the most extreme abuse for jumping up. If you can believe it, some Dark Side "training" texts recommend holding the dog's front paws, squeezing the paws, hitting the dog with a rolled-up newspaper, kneeing the dog in the chest, treading on its hind paws, or flipping it over backwards. And why? All because the dog wants to jump up to say hello in a manner that has, no doubt, been encouraged and condoned since puppyhood. And the dog's only crime? It grew! It is absolutely inhumane and irresponsible to allow a puppy to learn that it may derive affection from jumping up if you are going to punish the dog for the same behavior later in life. And it is also inhumane to physically torture the dog in that manner for any misbehavior. Why not just teach the puppydog how you would like it to greet people. For example, teach the dog to sit to say hello.

Jamie instructs Phoenie to "Sit-Stay" while greeting visitors.

From the outset, that is from the first day your puppy comes home, always have it sit when greeting people. You know the theory. It can't sit and jump up at the same time. Only it doesn't work anymore. Your cute cuddly pupski has collided headlong with adolescence and is so completely and utterly beside itself with excitement and eagerness to greet—yes, people!!!—that it hardly realizes you're on the same planet, let alone standing alongside issuing totally unheeded commands. Naughty, naughty owner! You should have paid heed to the advice in the Socialization chapter. You should always have had your puppy sit when greeting people. Well, don't worry, all is not lost. It's time to troubleshoot this problem once and for all.

First, let's make sure your dog knows how to greet you properly. On arriving home, request your dog to sit and do not say hello until it does. No matter how long it takes, ignore its eager bouncing and barking. Just wait for your dog to sit. When it finally does so, gently say hello, praise, and maybe offer a food reward. Give your dog the opportunity to sniff you over and get used to your presence. Then leave and come back home again. No matter how difficult or time-consuming the first homecoming, the second entry will be much easier. It will also take less time. So if you leave and come back yet again, you will see a similar further improvement. Each time you re-enter, your dog is less excited to see you and therefore easier to control. Let's face it: you may be the dog's owner, but if he's only just greeted you, he'll hardly be that excited to see you again just 20 seconds later. Continue with a series of re-entries until your dog eagerly sits and greets you perfectly in a courteous canine fashion.

Make sure your dog sits to greet visitors.

Yet Another Puppy Party?

Well, since you may have missed out on previous parties, it is now time for yet another Puppy Party. Invite twenty friends and teach the dog to adhere to the "sit to say hello" policy with each of them. Tonight, visitors are going to hand-feed your dog dinner at the front door. Have all visitors wait until your dog sits before petting your dog and offering a piece of kibble.

In the course of the party, have each visitor leave by the back door and re-enter by the front at least ten times. Make sure your dog sits each time it greets someone at the front door. With twenty guests, that's two hundred front door greetings you can practice at a single party. Some dogs sit out of sheer boredom! "Why waste energy jumping on someone you've just greeted four times in a row?" But most dogs sit because they want to. "You get treats for sitting!" This routine will probably generate a few interesting comments from visitors but then, hey!—their dogs probably still jump up.

While you've got volunteers at hand, have all the visitors walk in single file clockwise round the block five times, while you walk your dog round the block counterclockwise. In just five laps your dog can practice one hundred on-the-street encounters with ersatz strangers. The first lap is usually a bit hairy. The second is much better. But the third and subsequent laps are sit-city.

CHAPTER SEVEN

Six Basic Exercises

By now you will have realized that creating a True Companion Dog (TCD) comes down to six basic training exercises:

1 Socializing your dog to people (especially children, men, and strangers), other dogs, and other animals so that it learns good bite inhibition during play.

2 Housetraining your dog so it may live indoors instead of outdoors, and in your home instead of somebody else's.

3 Creating a chewtoy habit so your dog is profitably occupied chewing chewtoys, rather than destroying furniture and fittings, barking, or digging in the garden.

4 Teaching "Settle Down" and "Shush" so that little quiet moments become an integral part of your dog's day and are immediately available upon request.

5 Teaching your dog to sit willingly, promptly, and reliably so that among many other things, it does not jump on people.

6 Teaching your dog not to pull on leash, so that you and your dog may share many long walks together for a very long time. Regular walks are the very best way for your dog to meet and socialize with numerous unfamiliar people and dogs and so maintain its superior social skills.

If you have accomplished all of the above, "Congratulations!" You have a TCD, and you deserve a TCD. And you, are a TCP (True Companion Person). Your dog is extremely lucky to live with a good companion person like yourself. So why don't you raise your right hand (no, the other right hand) and pat yourself on the back and say "Well done! Good little dog owner!"

How to Teach A New Dog Old Tricks—Dr. Ian Dunbar

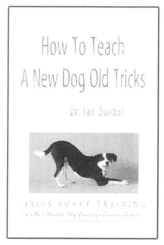

(192 pages)

Fun training with toys, treats, lures, and rewards. Easy, fun-loving, dog-friendly dog training methods for teaching a new puppy old tricks (such as basic manners), or for teaching an older dog who is new to training. The definitive text for lure/reward training techniques—written from the dog's point of view and emphasizing natural motivational methods to teach your dog to want to do what you want it to do!
Voted the #1 BEST BOOK by the Association of Pet Dog Trainers (1999).

SIRIUS® Puppy Training—Dr. Ian Dunbar

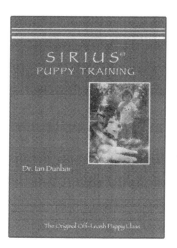

(90 minute DVD video)

Learn the gentle and enjoyable methods of off-leash socialization and training which made the SIRIUS® philosophy the international standard in pet dog training. SIRIUS® Puppy Training redefined and revolutionized dog training. SIRIUS® methods have been adopted and adapted by most progressive dog trainers worldwide. Before SIRIUS® there were no puppy classes, and virtually no food lures and rewards in dog training.
Voted the #1 BEST VIDEO (every year) by the Association of Pet Dog Trainers and by the Canadian Association of Professional Pet Dog Trainers.

CHAPTER EIGHT
Resources

To locate a Certified Pet Dog Trainer (CPDT) in your area contact: the Association of Pet Dog Trainers at:

1-800-PET-DOGS or online at www.apdt.com

The *GOOD LITTLE DOG BOOK* is to help puppy owners start off on the right foot (or paw). Curious puppy owners should watch the accompanying set of four *Training The Companion Dog* videos plus the *Training Dogs With Dunbar* video from the *Dogs With Dunbar* television series. More curious puppydog owners should read *How To Teach A New Dog Old Tricks* and watch *SIRIUS® Puppy Training*.

Books and videos are available online from:
www.jamesandkenneth.com

Training The Companion Dog—Dr. Ian Dunbar

*(Set of four 60 minute **DVD** videos)*

Winner of the Dog Writers' Association of America Award for Best Dog Training Video of the year. Topics include:
1. Socialization & Beginning Obedience. 2. Behavior Problems & Household Etiquette. 3. Walking On Leash. 4. Recalls & Stay.

Books and DVDs

Most bookshops and pet stores offer a bewildering choice of dog books and videos. Consequently, a number of dog-training organizations have voted on what they consider to be the most useful for prospective puppy owners. I have included some lists as voted by members of the Association of Pet Dog Trainers (APDT)— the largest association of pet dog trainers worldwide, and the dogSTAR daily staff. Most of the books and videos may be purchased from your local bookstore, or on-line from www.amazon.com.

APDT ALLTIME TOP TEN BEST DVDs

#1 **SIRIUS Puppy Training**
Dr. Ian Dunbar

#2 **Clicker Magic**
Karen Pryor

#3 **Take A Bow Wow**
Virginia Broitman & Sheri Lippman

#4 **Training The Companion Dog** (4 DVDs)
Dr. Ian Dunbar

#5 **Clicker Fun** (3 videos
Dr. Deborah Jones

#6 **Dog Aggression: Biting**
Dr. Ian Dunbar

#7 **The How of Bow Wow**
Virginia Broitman

#8 **Training Dogs With Dunbar**
Dr. Ian Dunbar

#9 **Calming Signals**
Turid Rugas

#10 **Puppy Love: Raise Your Dog The Clicker Way**
Karen Pryor & Carolyn Clark

dogSTARdaily's
TOP TEN BEST BOOKS
FOR PUPPY OWNERS

#1 How to Teach a New Dog Old Tricks - Ian Dunbar
James & Kenneth Publishers, 1991.

#2 Doctor Dunbar's Good Little Dog Book - Ian Dunbar
James & Kenneth Publishers, 1992.

#3 Your Outta Control Puppy - Teoti Anderson
TFH Publications Inc, 2003.

#4 Raising Puppies & Kids Together - Pia Silvani
TFH Publications Inc, 2005.

#5 The Perfect Puppy - Gwen Bailey
Hamlyn, 1995. (APDT #8)

#6 Dog Friendly Dog Training - Andrea Arden
IDG Books Worldwide, 2000.

#7 Positive Puppy Training Works - Joel Walton
David & James Publishers, 2002.

#8 The Power of Positive Dog Training - Pat Miller
Hungry Minds, 2001.

#9 25 Stupid Mistakes Dog Owners Make - Janine Adams
Lowell House, 2000.

#10 The Dog Whisperer - Paul Owens
Adams Media Corporation, 1999.

dogSTARdaily's
TOP TEN FUN BOOKS & DVDs

#1   Bow Wow Take 2 & **The How of Bow Wow** (2 videos)
Virginia Broitman. North Star Canines & Co. 1997.

#2   The Trick is in The Training - Stephanie Taunton & Cheryl
Smith. Barron's, 1998.

#3   Fun and Games with Your Dog - Gerd Ludwig
Barron's, 1996.

#4   Dog Tricks: Step by Step - Mary Zeigenfuse & Jan Walker
Howell Book House, 1997.

#5   Fun & Games with Dogs - Roy Hunter
Howlin Moon Press, 1993.

#6   Canine Adventures - Cynthia Miller
Animalia Publishing Company. 1999.

#7   Getting Started: Clicker Training for Dogs - Karen
Pryor. Sunshine Books, 2002

#8   Clicker Fun (3 videos) - Deborah Jones
Canine Training Systems, 1996.

#9   Agility Tricks - Donna Duford
Clean Run Productions, 1999.

#10 My Dog Can Do That!
ID Tag Company. 1991. The board game you play with your dog

dogSTARdaily's
CANINE CLASSICS

#1 The Culture Clash - Jean Donaldson
James & Kenneth Publishers, 1996.

#2 The Other End of The Leash - Patricia McConnell
Ballantine Books, 2002.

#3 Bones Would Rain From The Sky - Suzanne Clothier
Warner Books, 2002.

#4 *Excel*-erated Learning: Explaining How Dogs Learn and How Best to Teach Them - Pamela Reid
James & Kenneth Publishers, 1996.

#5 Don't Shoot the Dog - Karen Pryor
Bantam Books, 1985.

#6 Help For Your Fearful Dog - Nicole Wilde
Phantom Publishing, 2006.

#7 Behavior Problems in Dogs - William Campbell
Behavior Rx Systems, 1999.

#8 Biting & Fighting (2 DVDs) - Ian Dunbar
James & Kenneth Publishers, 2006.

#9 Dog Language - Roger Abrantes
Wakan Tanka Publishers, 1997.

#10 How Dogs Learn - Mary Burch & Jon Bailey
Howell Book House, 1999.

The Culture Clash—Jean Donaldson

The Culture Clash depicts dogs as they really are—stripped of their Hollywood fluff—with their loveable "can I eat it, chew it, urinate on it, what's in it for me" philosophy. Jean's tremendous affection for dogs shines through at all times, as does her keen insight into the dog's mind. Relentlessly she champions the dog's point of view, always showing concern for their education and well being.

Voted #1 Best Book by the Association of Pet Dog Trainers (2001) and Winner of the Dog Writers' Association of America Award for Best Dog Training Book. *(222 pages)*

Excel-erated Learning—Dr. Pamela Reid

A book that explains animal learning in a manner that is easily understood and entertaining. Learn the secrets for increasing the speed and efficiency of dog training. Understanding how dogs learn makes the process much easier and much more enjoyable for your dog. You'll be in a position to *excel*-erate your dog's learning!

Cutting-edge, scientific dog training techniques from agility enthusiast, obedience competitor, and psychologist Dr. Pamela Reid. *(174 pages)*

Veterinarian and animal behaviorist Dr. Ian Dunbar addresses the two most worrying behavior problems any dog owner can face—dogs that bite and dogs that fight. Dealing effectively with canine aggression necessitates a comprehensive understanding of its underlying causes.

BITING
(60 minute video seminar)

A thoughtful analysis of why dogs bite, outlining numerous preventative measures and a variety of practical remedial training techniques.

FIGHTING
(60 minute video seminar)

How to assess whether a dog has a serious and dangerous fighting problem or whether it is just prone to squabbling. How to resolve aggression and build up a dog's confidence and social contacts.

James & Kenneth Publishers   1 (800) 784-5531   www.jamesandkenneth.com

Every Picture Tells A Story—Dr. Ian Dunbar

(25 minute DVD video)

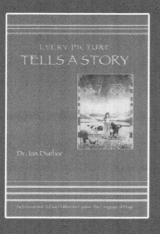

Dr. Ian Dunbar explores the relationship between children and dogs. Topics include: The language of dogs; Meeting strange dogs; Playing with dogs; Do you like dogs?; Teaching dogs our language; Scared dogs; Scary dogs; Good owners and good dogs; Clever dogs.

Dog Training for Children—Dr. Ian Dunbar

(84 minute DVD video)

Children have natural advantages as trainers. They are playful and fun and tend to coax and encourage, so dogs are happier to learn. This video will help children make the most of their natural talents, and prove that dog training is indeed child's play!

Topics include: Taking on a new puppy; Housetraining; Teaching sit, down, solid stays, and fast recalls; Focussing attention; Improving off-leash control; Developing a rapport; Training as a family; Teaching with toys and playing training games.

Dr. Ian Dunbar is a veterinarian, animal behaviorist, and author. He has written numerous books and hosted a dozen videos about puppydog behavior and training. *SIRIUS® Puppy Training* and *How To Teach A New Dog Old Tricks* were recently voted the #1 Best Video and #1 Best Book by the Association of Pet Dog Trainers. In his lifelong quest to promote owner-friendly and dog-friendly dog training, Dr. Dunbar has popularized the use of toys and treats and fun and games as lures and rewards. Dr. Dunbar is best known for his British television series *Dogs With Dunbar.* Ian lives in Berkeley, California with Kelly, Claude, and Ollie.

Bye!

Made in the USA
Charleston, SC
23 February 2013